Recruiting Minorities

What Explains Recent Trends in the Army and Navy?

Beth J. Asch, Paul Heaton, Bogdan Savych

Prepared for the Office of the Secretary of Defense

NATIONAL DEFENSE RESEARCH INSTITUTE

The research described in this report was prepared for the Office of the Secretary of Defense (OSD). The research was conducted in the RAND National Defense Research Institute, a federally funded research and development center sponsored by the OSD, the Joint Staff, the Unified Combatant Commands, the Department of the Navy, the Marine Corps, the defense agencies, and the defense Intelligence Community under Contract W74V8H-06-C-0002.

Library of Congress Cataloging-in-Publication Data

Asch, Beth J.
  Recruiting minorities : what explains recent trends in the Army and Navy? / Beth J. Asch, Paul Heaton, Bogdan Savych.
    p. cm.
  Includes bibliographical references.
  ISBN 978-0-8330-4717-5 (pbk. : alk. paper)
    1. United States. Army—Minorities. 2. United States. Navy—Minorities.
  3. United States. Army—Recruiting, enlistment, etc. 4. United States. Navy—Recruiting, enlistment, etc. I. Heaton, Paul. II. Savych, Bogdan. III. Title.

  UB417.A83 2009
  355.2'2308900973—dc22

                                                                    2009033157

The RAND Corporation is a nonprofit research organization providing objective analysis and effective solutions that address the challenges facing the public and private sectors around the world. RAND's publications do not necessarily reflect the opinions of its research clients and sponsors. **RAND**® is a registered trademark.

Published 2009 by the RAND Corporation
1776 Main Street, P.O. Box 2138, Santa Monica, CA 90407-2138
1200 South Hayes Street, Arlington, VA 22202-5050
4570 Fifth Avenue, Suite 600, Pittsburgh, PA 15213-2665
RAND URL: http://www.rand.org/
To order RAND documents or to obtain additional information, contact
Distribution Services: Telephone: (310) 451-7002;
Fax: (310) 451-6915; Email: order@rand.org

Preface

Since 2000, black enlistments have declined in the Army, as has the black share of high-quality Army enlistments. A recruit is deemed high-quality if he or she has a high school diploma and scores above average on the Armed Forces Qualification Test (AFQT). The decline in black enlistments is of concern to policymakers because the Army has struggled to meet its recruiting mission in recent years, and a significant decline in a key market segment represents a potential area for improvement. Furthermore, since the start of the all-volunteer force, Congress has been concerned about the degree to which military enlistments proportionately reflect the population that the U.S. military defends. At the same time that black representation among high-quality Army recruits has declined, Hispanic representation has increased. In addition, in comparison with the Army, black representation in the Navy has been stable, and Hispanic representation among high-quality Navy recruits has increased.

This report identifies factors that are correlated with trends in black and Hispanic representation among high-quality recruits in the Army and Navy, and it considers which policies are likely to be most effective in increasing high-quality enlistments among black, Hispanic, and white youth. The report also provides information on the relative cost-effectiveness of different resources among each market segment. The report should be of interest to policymakers concerned about military recruiting, and minority representation specifically, as well as defense manpower researchers.

This research was sponsored by the Office of Accession Policy within the Office of the Under Secretary of Defense for Personnel and Readiness and conducted within the Forces and Resource Policy Center of the RAND National Defense Research Institute, a federally funded research and development center sponsored by the Office of the Secretary of Defense, the Joint Staff, the Unified Combatant Commands, the Department of the Navy, the Marine Corps, the defense agencies, and the defense Intelligence Community.

For more information on RAND's Forces and Resources Policy Center, contact the director, James Hosek. He can be reached by email at James_Hosek@rand.org; by phone at 310-393-0411, extension 7183; or by mail at the RAND Corporation, 1776 Main Street, P.O. Box 2138, Santa Monica, California 90407-2138. More information about RAND is available at http://www.rand.org.

Contents

Figures

Tables

Summary

Since 2000, black enlistments into the Army have fallen precipitously. The number of black high-quality enlistments fell from 80 per 100,000 individuals in the U.S. population in July 2000 to 32 per 100,000 in July 2005. Although black high-quality enlistments have increased since 2005, they are still well below the 2000 level. Not only the number but also the percentage of recruits that are black has fallen in the Army. Black representation among high-quality Army recruits fell from 18.9 percent in 2000 to 10.6 percent in 2004, increasing to 11.8 percent in 2007. In contrast, black representation among high-quality Navy recruits over the same period has been generally stable.

The decline in black representation among high-quality Army enlistments is of concern because black youth are a key market segment for the Army, and the success of Army recruiting in the past is partially due to the ability of the Army to attract black youth into the military. Army recruiting has been challenging in recent years, and understanding why black enlistments have declined among high-quality Army enlistments is likely to be a component of the Army's strategy to meet its recruiting challenges. In addition, diversity of enlistments has been an area of concern among policymakers since the end of conscription in the United States in 1973: In that year, Congress mandated that the Department of Defense report the diversity of the armed forces annually.

In contrast to black enlistments, Hispanic representation among high-quality enlistments has increased since 2000 in both the Army and the Navy.[1] The Hispanic share of high-quality enlistments increased from 7.0 to 9.7 percent in the Army between 1999 and 2007, and from 9.6 to 15.4 percent in the Navy. For the Army, the key period of increase was between 2000 and 2003, when the Hispanic share increased by 3.3 percentage points, from 8.0 to 11.3. From 2003 to 2007, the Hispanic share fell to 9.7 percent. For the Navy, the key period of increase was between 2002 and 2005, when the Hispanic share rose from 10.9 to 16.2, or 5.3 percentage points. The disparate trends for Hispanic compared with black enlistments in the Army and Navy suggest that these market segments' enlistment decisions respond to different factors. That is, different market segments vary in their responses to resources, external opportunities, and other factors.

The research presented in this report was sponsored by the Office of the Under Secretary of Defense for Personnel and Readiness and was motivated by four research questions:

- What factors affect the enlistment supply of different market segments to the Army and Navy, and how do these effects differ by market segment and service?
- What factors explain changes in black and Hispanic representation among recruits? What explains the drop in black representation in the Army and the increase in Hispanic representation in the Army and Navy?
- How might policy changes affect the diversity of high-quality enlistments in terms of minority representation?
- Which policies are the most cost-effective?

---

[1]   Beginning January 1, 2003, the Office of Management and Budget implemented new guidance on the federal reporting of race and ethnicity. Prior to that date, Defense Manpower Data Center personnel data permitted categorization of race and ethnicity by first selection of all Hispanic records, and then sorting the balance of personnel records based on race category, thereby mixing up the race and ethnicity categorization. Beginning in January 2003, federal agencies, including DoD, collected and presented data that allowed identification of ethnicity ("Hispanic or Latino" and "Not Hispanic or Latino") separate from the identification of race.

For tabulations after January 2003, the definitions used in this report conform to the new guidance, but prior to that date they conform to the older guidance. This change does not affect our results, for reasons explained in Chapter Two.

Because the trends in representation differ for the Army and the Navy, these services offer benchmarks against which to compare the factors affecting the trends.

Approach

To address these questions, we estimate enlistment supply models for black, Hispanic, and white youth for the Army and for the Navy. The models show the relationship between, on the one hand, the number of high-quality enlistments in a quarter and in a state and, on the other hand, factors thought to affect supply (recruiting resources, military pay, and civilian opportunities, including civilian pay and college); factors related to enlistment eligibility, such as obesity rates; and political factors (specifically, the Iraq war). We use enlistment data obtained from the Army and the Navy, covering the period 1998 through 2007 for the Army and 1999 through 2007 for the Navy. We merge these data with data on recruiters from the services, data on demographic and economic factors from the Current Population Survey (CPS) and other nonmilitary data, and data on casualties and presidential polls. We estimate enlistment models by state and quarter. While we estimate models for both the Army and the Navy, we do not estimate cross-service effects. That is, we do not estimate joint Army and Navy enlistment models by race and ethnicity. Also, our models capture associations between the factors and enlistments rather than causal relationships. Some of the associations may reflect factors that are unmeasured within the models.

After estimating each model for each service, we use the models to decompose the underlying factors associated with the change in black representation in the Army and the change in Hispanic representation in the Army and in the Navy. These changes can be due to differences in the responsiveness of different market segments to the factors associated with enlistment supply and to variation in how these factors changed over time.

Responsiveness to Resources

We find that the market segments differ in their responsiveness to some recruiting resources in the Army. More specifically, we estimate that black Army high-quality enlistments increase more with recruiters than they do with enlistment bonuses, military pay relative to civilian pay, and educational benefits. For example, we find that a 10 percent increase in Army recruiters is associated with a 6.2 percent increase in Army black high-quality enlistments, whereas a 10 percent increase in enlistment bonuses is associated with a 2.0 percent increase in black high-quality Army enlistments. The estimated effects of military pay and educational benefits on black Army enlistments are not statistically significantly different from zero.

We estimate that Hispanic high-quality Army enlistments are highly responsive to military pay as well as to Army educational benefits and recruiters, but are less responsive to Army enlistment bonuses. According to our estimates, a 10 percent increase in relative military pay is associated with a 23.5 percent increase in Hispanic Army high-quality enlistments, whereas a 10 percent increase in enlistment bonuses is associated with a 1.3 percent increase in Hispanic high-quality enlistments.

In the case of the Navy, we estimate that both black and Hispanic high-quality enlistments are responsive to Navy recruiters. The estimated effects of bonuses, military pay, and educational benefits were not statistically different from zero. For recruiters, we estimate that a 10 percent increase in Navy recruiters is associated with a 5.4 percent increase in black enlistments and a 5.7 percent increase in Hispanic enlistments.

We also find that enlistments respond differently to resources in the Army versus the Navy. In general, Navy responsiveness to resources is lower, in percentage terms, than Army responsiveness. For example, a 10 percent increase in recruiters is estimated to increase Army high-quality enlistments by 6.2 percent for blacks and 7.9 percent for Hispanics, whereas for the Navy these figures are both below 6 percent.

Accounting for Recent Changes in Minority Representation

When we decompose the changes in the representation of blacks and Hispanics among high-quality recruits over time using our estimated models, we estimate that the 8.3 percentage point drop in black Army representation between the fourth quarters of 2000 and 2004 can be attributed to a large negative effect of the Iraq war on black enlistments and the success of the Army in recruiting high-quality youth among the Hispanic and white populations. The Iraq war was associated with a negative effect for all market segments, but the effect was largest for blacks—45 percent versus 21 percent for whites and Hispanics—over our data period. On the other hand, black enlistments were more insensitive to the large increases in regular military compensation relative to civilian pay that occurred over this period, compared with white and Hispanic enlistments. Consequently, part of the decline in black representation appears to be due to the success of the Army in increasing Hispanic and white enlistments, and therefore their market share, via increases in military pay.

When we decompose the 3.3 percentage point increase in Army Hispanic high-quality enlistments between 2000 and 2003, we find that increases in the Montgomery GI Bill explain about a third of the increase, or 1.4 percentage points. Increases in military pay, and the stronger responsiveness of Hispanic than black youth to increases in relative military pay, explain almost a quarter of the increase in Hispanic representation over this period. Since white Army enlistments are also highly responsive to increases in relative military pay, the increase in white enlistments had an offsetting effect on Hispanic representation. Thus, resource changes have been important in explaining improvements in Hispanic representation in the Army in recent years.

Hispanic representation among high-quality Navy recruits has also increased, rising by 5.3 percentage points between 2002 and 2005. The majority of this increase—5 percentage points—is attributable to the positive estimated effect of the Iraq war on Hispanic enlistments in our Navy model. We estimate that the Iraq war has a larger positive effect on Hispanic than black enlistments, and a negative effect on white enlistments. Thus, as the Iraq war progressed over this period, the Hispanic share rose dramatically in response. The underlying cause of the Iraq war's positive effects for black and Hispanic Navy recruiting is unclear. One possibility is that minority youth who would like to serve in the military are choosing the Navy over the Army.

Policy Implications

Our analysis suggests that the key factors explaining the changes in black high-quality enlistment in the Army are the Iraq war and the rise in Hispanic representation among high-quality Army enlistments due to the greater responsiveness of Hispanics to military pay, relative to civilian pay, and to educational benefits. In the case of the Navy, we estimate that most of the rise in Hispanic representation among Navy high-quality enlistments is attributable to the positive effect of the Iraq war on Navy Hispanic enlistments that exceeded the positive effect of the Iraq war on black enlistments and the negative effect of the Iraq war on white enlistments.

Our model suggests that high-quality black enlistments will not continue to decline going forward due to effects of the Iraq war. Whether black high-quality enlistments will recover following a drawdown depends on whether the war had temporary or permanent effects on attitudes toward enlistment among high-quality youth. Similarly, whether the positive effect on Navy enlistments during the Iraq war on Hispanic and black high-quality enlistments will continue or reverse depends on whether these are permanent or temporary effects. These are open questions.

Our estimates indicate that recruiters best increase black high-quality enlistments into the Army when compared with bonuses and relative military pay. We also estimate recruiters to be more effective than other resources in increasing black Navy high-quality enlistments. With respect to Hispanic high-quality enlistments, we find that this segment is more responsive to military pay in the Army, as well as to recruiters and educational benefits, than it is to enlistment bonuses. For the Navy, we find that Hispanic high-quality enlistments are responsive to recruiters. Finally, the estimates indicate that white enlistments in both the Navy and Army are more responsive to military pay and recruiters than to educational benefits and bonuses.

Given the differential responsiveness of different market segments to recruiting resources, the analysis suggests the opportunity to target resources to specific market segments in each service, and even across services. However, such an approach to recruiting resource policy may run counter to notions of equity and fairness. That is, the services might be reluctant to target resources based on race and ethnicity. Still, as decisions are made about the allocation of resources to different policies, it could be useful for the services to recognize that such allocation decisions will have an effect not only on the quantity of high-quality enlistments but also on their distribution across market segments, and these effects could alter the representation of different segments. The analysis also suggests the possibility of targeting resources across services by market segment, given the differential responses of different market segments across services. Because we do not estimate a joint model of Army and Navy enlistments, we do not address the question of resource allocation across services; such analysis should be explored in future research. Still, the analysis indicates that increasing minority representation in the overall military could involve a cross-service strategy.

Acknowledgments

We are grateful to the U.S. Army Accessions Command for its help in answering questions and providing data. Specifically, we would like to thank Claudia Tamplin, Kevin Lyman, Donald Bohn, and MAJ Trevor Dison. We are also grateful to John Noble at the Navy Recruiting Command for his support for our project. We also received help and data from others at the Navy Recruiting Command, and we would like to thank Rich Van Meter, Robert Phillips, Michael Evans, and Gary Ton. We are indebted to the Defense Manpower Data Center and Richard Moreno for their help in providing data and answering questions. We also are grateful for the advice, guidance, and data we received from our colleague John Warner at Clemson University. At RAND, we are grateful to James Dertouzos for constructive comments on our work and to Janet Hanley for working with us to provide an analysis file. We also thank, without naming, the many individuals at RAND who provided comments and observations in the RAND Defense Manpower Seminar and participants of the Western Economics Association meetings. We thank James Hosek for his support and input to our project, and the two RAND reviewers who provided excellent comments that improved the quality of the report, Nicholas Burger and Sebastian Negrusa. Finally, we are deeply grateful for the support, patience, and farsightedness of our project sponsor, Curtis Gilroy, Director, Accession Policy, and for the help we received from those who work in his office, especially John Jessup, Christopher Arendt, Dennis Drogo, and Robert Clark in the Office of Accession Policy within the Office of the Under Secretary of Defense (Personnel and Readiness).

Abbreviations

AFQT	Armed Forces Qualification Test
CPS	Current Population Survey
DMDC	Defense Manpower Data Center
FY	fiscal year
MGIB	Montgomery GI Bill
OSD	Office of the Secretary of Defense
Q1	first quarter of fiscal year
Q2	second quarter of fiscal year
Q3	third quarter of fiscal year
Q4	fourth quarter of fiscal year

CHAPTER ONE

Introduction

It is well known among the policy community and general public that the Army has had recruiting challenges in recent years. Articles in the popular press have focused on the Army's difficulty in meeting recruiting goals, as reported in the *Washington Post* (Tyson, 2005), and on the greater use of waivers, as reported in the *New York Times* (Alvarez, 2007). While the causes of these challenges are multiple and complex, two key factors appear to be rising college attendance among recent high school graduates and the Iraq war's negative effects on enlistment. Simon and Warner (2007) find that by 2005, each year of the Iraq war was associated with a 34 percent decline in high-quality enlistments.[1] In contrast to the Army, the Navy has met its enlistment goals in recent years, and Navy recruit quality has remained high, as will be shown in greater detail below.

Less widely reported has been a dramatic drop in the representation of blacks among high-quality Army recruits. Black representation among high-quality Army gross contracts fell between fiscal years (FYs) 2000 and 2004, from 18.9 to 10.6 percent.[2] In contrast to the

---

[1] A recruit is deemed high-quality if he or she has a high school diploma and scores above average on the Armed Forces Qualification Test (AFQT).

[2] Individuals who enter the military sign an enlistment contract. Those who sign a contract to arrive at boot camp at a later date in the year enter what is known as the Delayed Entry Program. Gross contracts are the number of contracts signed in a given month. Net contracts are gross contracts minus the number of individuals who drop out from the Delayed Entry Program. Our analysis focuses on gross high-quality contracts. We use the terms "contracts," "enlistments," and "recruits" interchangeably throughout the report.

Army, black representation among Navy enlistment contracts has been generally stable.

The decline in black representation among Army enlistments is cause for concern for two reasons. First, representation of minorities among recruits has been a concern of policymakers since the draft debates in the late 1960s, when some proponents of the draft expressed concern that an all-volunteer force would increase black representation in combat-related assignments and ultimately in combat-related casualties (Binkin and Eitelberg, 1982). Although the Gates Commission report of 1970 argued for the end of the draft and predicted that the all-volunteer force would not change social representation, Congress mandated in 1974 that the Department of Defense provide statistics on the annual social representation of the armed forces, including enlistments, in terms of such characteristics as race, ethnicity, marital status, and age (Senate Armed Services Committee, 1974). The second reason is that blacks represent a key market segment for the Army in terms of meeting its recruiting mission. A precipitous decline means that the Army has lost market share. To reverse the declines in Army high-quality enlistments and successfully meeting its recruiting challenges, the Army must improve its success rate among key demographic groups, including blacks.

This report addresses several research questions related to recent trends in social representation:

- What factors affect the enlistment supply of different market segments to the Army and Navy, and how do these effects differ by market segment and service?
- What factors explain changes in black and Hispanic representation among recruits? What explains the drop in black representation in the Army and the increase in Hispanic representation in the Army and Navy?
- How might policy changes affect the diversity of high-quality enlistments in terms of minority representation?
- Which policies are the most cost-effective?

To address these questions, our project estimated enlistment supply models of high-quality recruiting, by race and ethnicity, for the Army and the Navy. The focus on these two services is based on a request from the project sponsor. Because the Army representation of blacks has declined sharply while Navy representation has been relatively stable, the Army and Navy provide contrasting pictures of the trends in black representation and, potentially, the factors that affect these trends.

The Army and the Navy provided individual-level enlistment data for their respective services, as well as data on recruiters and missions, and we supplemented these data with information on demographic and economic trends from various sources, such as the Current Population Survey (CPS) and the U.S. Census. Though the enlistment data were provided at the individual recruit level, we aggregate the data by quarter and state and estimate aggregate enlistment models. Such models are well suited for estimating the relationship between enlistments and variables that vary by time (such as military pay), variables that vary by geographic area, and those that vary by time and area. The data span the period 1998 through 2007 for the Army and 1999 through 2007 for the Navy.

The report is organized as follows. Chapter Two provides background information on trends in Army and Navy high-quality enlistments, particularly the representation of minorities among recruits, and on trends in recruiting resources. Chapter Three presents the econometric modeling approach we use and discusses the data in more detail. Chapter Four presents our Army results, while Chapter Five presents our Navy results. Chapter Six presents the conclusions and policy implications.

CHAPTER TWO

Background on Recruiting

This chapter reports recent trends in Army and Navy enlistments, by market segment, as well as trends in factors that may affect enlistments, such as recruiting resources, economic trends, and demographic factors. The trends show the changes in minority representation among high-quality recruits in the Army and the Navy and the changes the Army and Navy made to recruiting resources in recent years. Past research shows that demographic and economic factors affect recruiting outcomes, so this chapter also shows changes in such factors as the unemployment rate and veterans' population.

Trends in Enlistments

Trends in Army Enlistments

Evidence demonstrating the recruiting challenges facing the Army is shown in Figures 2.1 and 2.2. Figure 2.1 shows that, following an increase in recruit quality (as measured by the AFQT) between 2001 and 2004, recruit quality fell by 2007. The percentage of Army contracts with an AFQT score above 50, which places recruits in AFQT categories I to IIIA, fell between 2004 and 2007, from 72 percent to 60 percent, while the percentage scoring in AFQT IV, the lowest level allowed by Congress, and capped by Congress at 4 percent of enlistments, rose from 1.3 percent to 3.8 percent between these years. Figure 2.1 also shows that the education level among recruits declined. The percentage of recruits who were high school graduates fell from 89 to 75 between 2004 and 2007. Figure 2.2 shows a

Figure 2.1
Percentage of Army Gross Contracts, by AFQT Category and High School Graduation Status

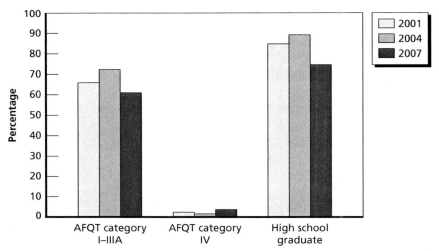

SOURCE: Authors' calculations based on Army recruiting data.
RAND *MG861-2.1*

substantial increase in the proportion of recruits who received waivers for failing to meet at least one enlistment standard. The percentage of Army contracts with waivers rose from 14 percent in 2004 to 20 percent in 2007. Furthermore, the Army enlisted more recruits who were obese, which is defined as having a body mass index above 30. The percentage of recruits having a body mass index above 30 increased from 8 percent in 2004 to 12 percent in 2007.

The decline in recruit quality shown in Figure 2.1 is proportional among market segments. That is, the percentage of Army contracts that are considered high-quality follows the same pattern whether we consider white, black, or Hispanic contracts, as shown in Figure 2.3.[1]

_____

[1]   Beginning January 1, 2003, the Office of Management and Budget implemented new guidance on the federal reporting of race and ethnicity. Prior to that date, Defense Manpower Data Center personnel data permitted categorization of race and ethnicity by first selection of all Hispanic records, and then sorting the balance of personnel records based on race category, thereby mixing up the race and ethnicity categorization. Beginning in January 2003, federal agencies, including DoD, collected and presented data that allowed identifi-

Figure 2.2
Percentage of Army Gross Contracts, by Waiver and Body Mass Index Status

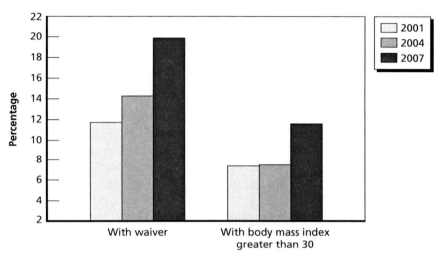

SOURCE: Authors' calculations based on Army recruiting data.
RAND *MG861-2.2*

The percentage declines by about 28 percent, regardless of market segment.

Though the percentage of black contracts that are high-quality follows a pattern similar to that of Hispanics and whites, the percentage of total high-quality contracts that are black dropped precipitously,

---

cation of ethnicity ("Hispanic or Latino" and "Not Hispanic or Latino") separate from the identification of race.

For tabulations after January 2003, the definitions used in this report conform to the new guidance, but prior to that date they conform to the older guidance. This change does not affect our results, for three reasons. First, we separately observe both race and ethnicity from two different data sources for the Army, the Army REQUEST data and the DoD MEPCOM data, so we do not have to rely on the Army's coding of people into a single race. Second, because we include state and time effects in our estimated models, we identify the effects of variables such as recruiters and bonuses on minority enlistments based on differences in contract trends within states over time. It is unlikely that the change in the definition of race and ethnicity in 2003 would affect differences in trends across states. Finally, as will be discussed in Chapter Two, we observe relatively little change in the representation of Hispanics and blacks among high-quality Army recruits between 2002 and 2003, so the magnitude of any effect of the definition change on or results is likely to be small.

Figure 2.3
Percentage of White, Black, and Hispanic Army Gross Contracts That Are High-Quality

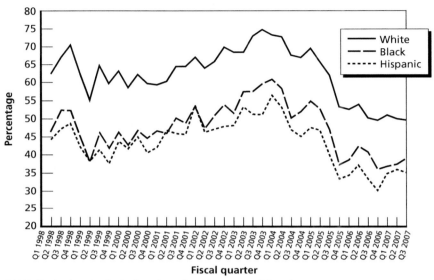

SOURCE: Authors' calculations based on Army recruiting data.

RAND *MG861-2.3*

as shown in Figure 2.4. The percentage fell from 18.9 percent in the fourth quarter of FY2000 ("Q4 2000") to 10.6 percent in Q4 2004, a decline of more than 8 percentage points. Interestingly, the drop began in 2000, before the attacks of September 11, 2001. Thus, some of the factors that affect black representation must have changed, even before the change in the national security environment in September 2001.

Figure 2.5 shows the pattern in percentage of high-quality contracts that are Hispanic. Figure 2.6 shows the pattern for whites. Hispanic representation among high-quality Army contracts increased substantially between Q2 1999 and Q4 2003, rising from 6.8 to 11.3 percent. The primary period of increase was between Q1 2000 and Q4 2003, when the Hispanic share of high-quality enlistments increased by 3.3 percentage points from 8.0 to 11.3 percent. However, since 2003, Hispanic representation has trended downward, falling to 9.1 percent by Q2 2007. White representation among high-quality

Figure 2.4
Percentage of Army High-Quality Gross Contracts That Are Black

Fiscal quarter

SOURCE: Authors' calculations based on Army recruiting data.
RAND *MG861-2.4*

contracts increased between Q3 1999 and Q4 2005, from 69.5 percent to 75.3 percent. Since 2005, white representation has been stable.

A different way to observe the decline in black representation among high-quality Army recruits is to consider the trend in numbers of high-quality contracts, by market segment, shown in Figure 2.7. While high-quality contracts dropped among all market segments between 2002 and 2005, the drop among black high-quality contracts was disproportionately greater. Thus, the decline in black representation between 2003 and 2005 is not due to increases in Hispanic and white high-quality enlistment supply, because supply for these market segments also declined. Rather, it is due to factors that disproportionately affected black supply relative to white and Hispanic supply.

Figure 2.5
Percentage of Army High-Quality Gross Contracts That Are Hispanic

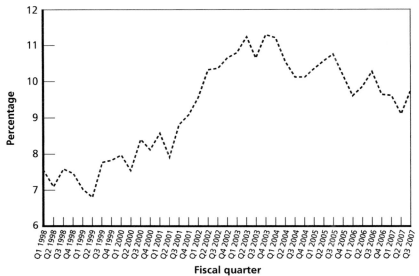

SOURCE: Authors' calculations based on Army recruiting data.
RAND *MG861-2.5*

Trends in Navy Enlistments

Black high-quality contracts for the Navy show a different pattern than for the Army. Instead of dropping dramatically, black high-quality contracts have been fairly stable in the Navy, as shown in Figures 2.8 and 2.9. Figure 2.8 shows black and Hispanic representation among Navy high-quality contracts, and Figure 2.9 shows the trend in the number of Navy high-quality contracts by market segment. The Navy enlisted about 1,000 to 1,200 black high-quality recruits per quarter in 1998. Furthermore, Hispanic high-quality contracts have increased steadily since 1998, rising from a seasonally adjusted count of 685 contracts per quarter in the second quarter of FY1999 to 1,206 per quarter in the third quarter of FY2007, or by 76 percent. Hispanic representation among high-quality Navy contracts increased between 1999 and 2007 from 9.6 to 15.4 percent. The primary period of increase was between Q4 2002 and Q4 2005, when

Figure 2.6
Percentage of Army High-Quality Gross Contracts That Are White

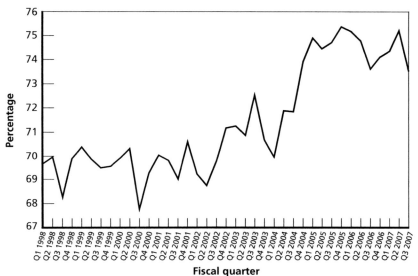

SOURCE: Authors' calculations based on Army recruiting data.
RAND MG861-2.6

the Hispanic share of high-quality enlistments increased by 5.3 percentage points from 10.9 to 16.2 percent, as shown in Figure 2.8.

Figure 2.9 reveals that the market segment with the most substantial enlistment variation is whites (measured along the right axis rather than the left axis), among whom there was a substantial decline in enlistments between 2002 and 2005, followed by a recovery in later years. Overall, high-quality enlistments declined from a peak of over 9,100 in Q4 2002 to just over 6,000 three-and-one-quarter years later, in Q1 2006 (data not shown in Figure 2.9). The Navy recruiting from Q1 2006 through 2007 represents an important success story, with quarterly recruit counts recovering to roughly 7,500 enlistments per quarter.

Figure 2.7
Army High-Quality Gross Contracts per 100,000 Population

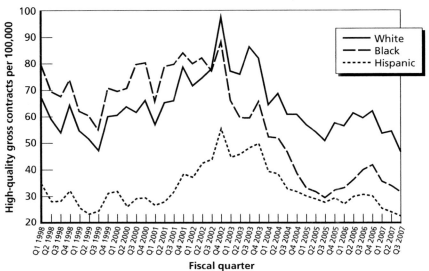

SOURCE: Authors' calculations based on Army recruiting data.
RAND MG861-2.7

Also in contrast to the Army, for which the percentage of gross contracts that are high-quality declined for all market segments (Figure 2.3), the percentage increased in the Navy, as shown in Figure 2.10. Between Q3 2000 and Q3 2007, the percentages increased by about 15 percentage points for Hispanics and blacks and by about 10 percentage points for whites. Together, Figures 2.9 and 2.10 show that the Navy was able to simultaneously increase both the absolute numbers of recruits and average recruit quality between 2006 and 2007. Unsurprisingly, given the patterns in Figure 2.10, the black share of high-quality enlistments has remained relatively steady, while Hispanics have increased share over this period.

Figure 2.8
Percentage of Navy High-Quality Gross Contracts That Are Black, Hispanic

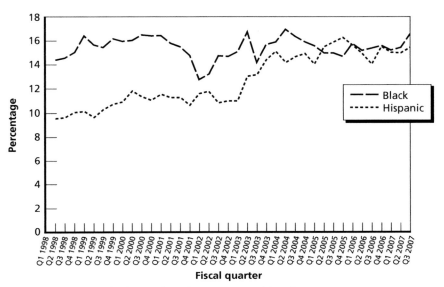

SOURCE: Authors' calculations based on Navy recruiting data.
RAND *MG861-2.8*

Trends in Factors That May Affect Enlistments

Past studies find that recruiting resources, as well as economic, demographic, and political factors (such as the Iraq war), affect enlistment supply. We discuss the previous literature in the next chapter. In this subsection, we first present trends in recruiting resources for the Army and Navy. We then discuss economic trends that could affect civilian opportunities outside the military, demographic trends that could affect the eligibility of the population for enlistment, and political factors, particularly the Iraq war.

Figure 2.9
Navy High-Quality Gross Contracts, by Market Segment

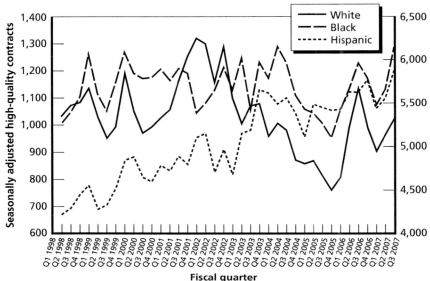

Fiscal quarter

SOURCE: Authors' calculations based on Navy recruiting data.
NOTE: The figures along the left y-axis indicate the number of seasonally adjusted
high-quality contracts for blacks and Hispanics; the numbers along the right y-axis
indicate these numbers for whites (on a greater scale).
RAND *MG861-2.9*

Trends in Recruiting Resources

Figures 2.11–2.16 depict recent trends in a variety of resources used
by the Army to promote enlistments, including recruiters, enlistment
bonuses, and recruiter enlistment goals. The pre-9/11 period was one
of relative stability in resources, with goals declining slowly, recruiter
force size remaining roughly constant, and enlistment bonuses rising
gradually. Perhaps surprisingly, the commencement of hostilities in
Iraq also coincided with a substantial decrease in enlistment objectives
for the Army—between Q2 2003 and Q3 2004, the Army's contract
goal fell from 98,000 to 75,000, a decrease of almost 25 percent, as
shown in Figure 2.11.

Figure 2.10
**Percentage of White, Black, and Hispanic Navy Gross Contracts That Are
High-Quality**

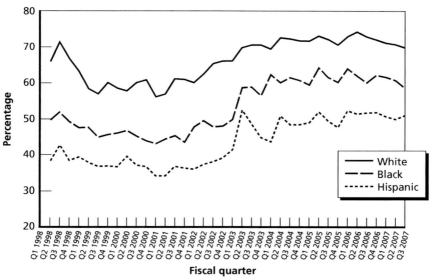

SOURCE: Authors' calculations based on Navy recruiting data.
RAND *MG861-2.10*

Commensurate with the changes in the contract mission, recruiter counts as well as average bonuses dropped during this period. Figure 2.12 indicates that declines were particularly acute among the recruiter force, a traditionally high-yield resource that fell by more than 20 percent over this period. Faced with the increased manpower needs associated with continuing large-scale operations in Iraq and Afghanistan, the Army significantly upwardly adjusted goals and resources beginning in the latter part of 2004.

Figure 2.11
Annual Army Contract Goal

SOURCE: Authors' calculations based on Army recruiting data.
RAND *MG861-2.11*

An important trend during this resource-expansion period was the increased use of enlistment bonuses as a recruitment tool. By the first half of 2006, enlistment bonus levels were substantially above levels typically observed over the past decade, with averages reaching above $8,000 per new contract, as shown in Figure 2.13. Although average enlistment bonuses moderated somewhat between Q2 2006 and Q1 2007, they remain above historic levels.[2] Over the final 1.5 years of the sample, the size of the Army recruiter force stabilized just above 6,000.

---

[2]   Although our analysis ends in Q3 2007 due to availability of some variables, it is noteworthy that enlistment bonuses more than doubled in Q4 2007 as the Army pushed to meet recruiting targets for FY2007.

Figure 2.12
Trend in Army Production Recruiters

Fiscal quarter

SOURCE: Authors' calculations based on Army recruiting data.
RAND *MG861-2.12*

In addition to those incentives controlled directly by the Army, military-wide enlistment incentives experienced important shifts during our sample period. Figures 2.14 and 2.15 plot the trends in educational benefits and regular military compensation, respectively, for a new recruit in the first year. The primary military educational incentive program is the Montgomery GI Bill (MGIB), which is available to active duty members of all military branches and provides monthly payments for educational expenses. Maximum MGIB benefit generosity increased by approximately 75 percent between 2000 and 2003, far outpacing increases in average college tuition during this period.[3] Figure 2.15 also demonstrates that regular military

---

[3] For obvious reasons, military advertisements and recruiters emphasize maximum benefit levels to potential recruits, although many enlistees ultimately receive only a fraction of their potential benefit. Negrusa, Warner, and Simon (2007) provide more information on MGIB utilization patterns.

Figure 2.13
Trend in Average Army Enlistment Bonuses

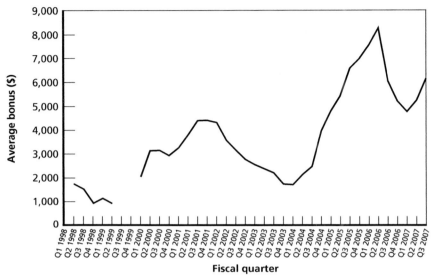

SOURCE: Authors' calculations based on Army recruiting data.
NOTE: We are missing data for the second and third quarters of FY1999.
RAND MG861-2.13

compensation increased by over 10 percent in real terms at the beginning of 2001 and then, after remaining flat for the next five years,
increased again in FY2006–2007.

Figure 2.14
Trend in Maximum Montgomery GI Bill Benefit

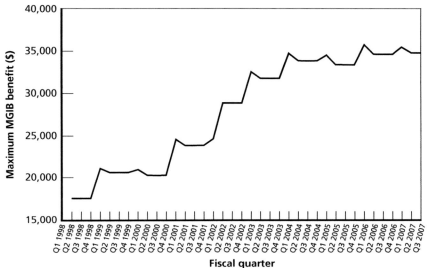

SOURCE: DoD Actuary.
RAND MG861-2.14

Individual services have also instituted College Fund programs that provide additional, supplemental educational payments to eligible high-quality recruits who enter hard-to-fill occupational areas. Given the substantial increases in MGIB benefit generosity documented in Figure 2.15, Army and Navy College Fund programs were scaled back between 2000 and 2004.[4] Figure 2.16 demonstrates that Army College Fund offer rates have recovered somewhat since 2004, although this incentive remains available to a relatively small proportion of the total incoming group of recruits.

---

[4] The declining importance of college funds as a recruitment tool has coincided with the introduction of new incentives, such as the Navy Loan Repayment Program and the Army Advantage Fund.

Figure 2.15
Trend in Regular Military Compensation for First-Year Recruits

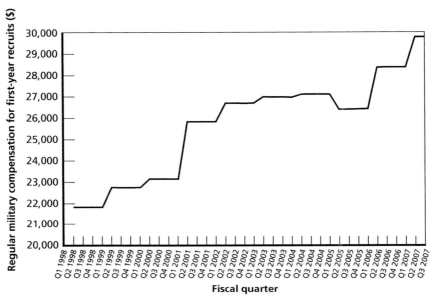

SOURCE: Office of Compensation, Office of the Under Secretary of Defense
(Personnel and Readiness).
RAND MG861-2.15

Trends in Navy Recruiting Resources

Figures 2.17–2.20 plot quarterly measures of recruiting resources for the
Navy between 1999 and 2007. Figure 2.18 shows that Navy recruiter
counts, after initially remaining relatively flat, declined steadily during
FY2002–FY2005 before rebounding somewhat through 2007. In
response to the more difficult recruiting environment associated
with continuing military operations in Iraq and Afghanistan, Navy
enlistment bonuses increased substantially between 2005 and 2007,
as shown in Figure 2.19. In contrast to bonuses, college funds have
become a less important enlistment incentive over time, falling from a
peak receipt rate of roughly 20 percent in 2001 to less than 5 percent
of enlistees at the end of the sample (Figure 2.20). The declining use of

Figure 2.16
Fraction of Army Recruits Receiving the Army College Fund Benefit

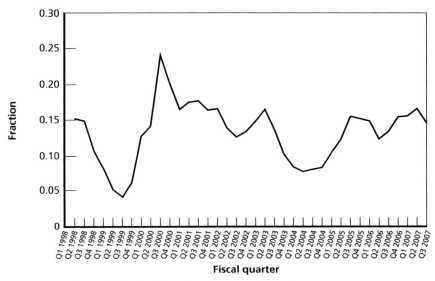

SOURCE: Authors' calculations based on Army recruiting data.
RAND *MG861-2.16*

college funds as an enlistment incentive partly reflects sharp increases in the value of the MGIB program (Figure 2.14) that have affected all services. In addition, the Navy introduced a competing incentive in the form of the Navy Loan Repayment Program in 2003, although the scale of this program remains small.

Figure 2.17
Annual Navy Contract Goal

SOURCE: Authors' calculations based on Navy recruiting data.
RAND MG861-2.17

Economic Factors

Military pay relative to civilian pay has increased in recent years. Figure 2.21 shows the growth in civilian earnings by presenting an index of civilian earnings of high school graduates, measured as civilian earnings in a given quarter relative to earnings in the first quarter of 1996. Thus, the chart shows growth relative to the beginning of 1996. To smooth the trends, we present the index of a three-month moving average of civilian earnings, by race and ethnicity. The data used are the monthly CPS data.

Figure 2.18
Trend in Navy Production Recruiters

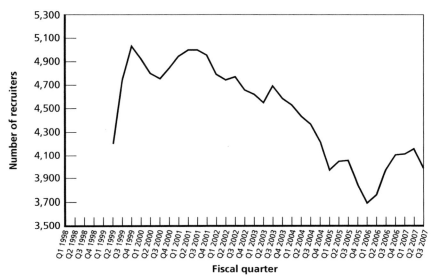

SOURCE: Authors' calculations based on Navy recruiting data.
RAND *MG861-2.18*

We find that, among full-time high school graduates age 18 to
40, full-time civilian earnings increased between 1996 and early 2000
for whites, Hispanics, and blacks. Beginning in 2000, the growth in
Hispanic civilian earnings slowed, and even declined between 2000
and 2001; but by 2007, Hispanic civilian earnings were 7.1 percent
higher than they were in 1996. Growth in civilian earnings for whites
stabilized by 2001, and civilian earnings for white high school graduates were relatively constant between 2000 and 2005 at about 6 or
7 percent, declining to 5 percent by 2007. For black high school graduates, civilian earnings continued to grow from 2000 through 2002,
but declined between 2004 and 2005, returning to the 2000 level in
2005. By 2007, civilian earnings for each market segment were about
7 percent higher than in 1996.

Figure 2.19
Trend in Average Navy Enlistment Bonuses

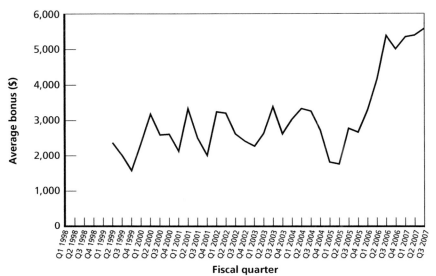

SOURCE: Authors' calculations based on Navy recruiting data.
RAND MG861-2.19

Civilian earnings capture one facet of the civilian alternatives available to those who might enlist. The civilian unemployment rate captures expected job opportunities. Past studies find that high-quality enlistments are positively associated with increases in the civilian unemployment rate.

Figure 2.20
Percentage of Navy Recruits Receiving the Navy College Fund

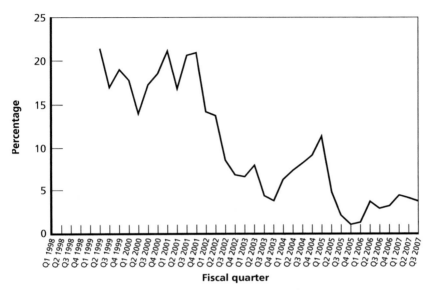

SOURCE: Authors' calculations based on Navy recruiting data.
RAND *MG861-2.20*

Figure 2.22 shows trends in the civilian unemployment rate of high school graduates, age 18 to 40, by race and ethnicity, obtained from processing the CPS data. The unemployment rate is higher among black than among Hispanics or whites. Until 2002, the Hispanic unemployment rate was greater than that for whites. However, the two rates converge by 2002.

Figure 2.21
Index of Civilian Weekly Full-Time Earnings of High School Graduates, by Race/Ethnicity, by Quarter, 1 = 1st Quarter 1996, Three-Month Moving Average

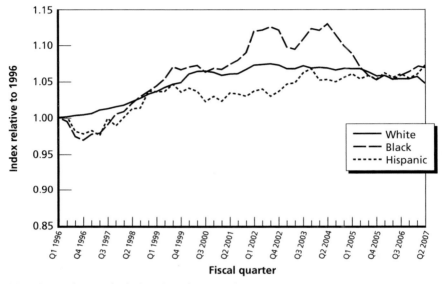

SOURCE: Authors' calculations based on CPS data.
RAND MG861-2.21

The unemployment rate follows similar trends over time for all market segments. The unemployment rate declined during the booming economy of the late 1990s, especially for Hispanics and blacks, falling, for example, from 9.5 percent for Hispanics in 1996 to 5.7 percent at the end of 2000. Unemployment rates began to rise in mid-2001 for whites, and later in 2001 for blacks and Hispanics, as the U.S. economy experienced a recession. The rate increased more for whites than Hispanics, so that, by 2002, white and Hispanic high school graduates had nearly the same unemployment rate. Beginning in 2004, the unemployment rate for each market segment began to decline, although the magnitude of the decline differs across segments.

Figure 2.22
**Civilian Unemployment Rate of High School Graduates, by Race/Ethnicity,
by Quarter**

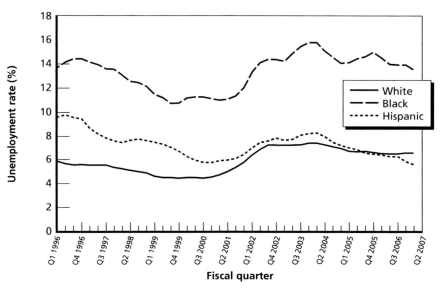

SOURCE: Authors' calculations based on CPS data.
RAND *MG861-2.22*

Demographic Factors

Demographic factors may affect enlisted supply in a number ways. First, they may affect individuals' propensity to enlist. For example, the size of different segments of the influencer population, such as the veterans' population, affect propensity to enlist (see, for example, Warner, Simon, and Payne, 2001). Some demographic factors may affect the likelihood that individuals will qualify for enlistment, such as the obesity rate. Other factors can affect both the propensity to enlist and qualification rates. For example, individuals who are not U.S. citizens are less likely to qualify for enlistment, but military service provides an avenue toward accelerated citizenship, so noncitizens may be more inclined to enlist than citizens. Similarly, individuals who engage in criminal activity are less likely to be eligible to enlist, but individuals who live in crime-ridden neighborhoods may have a greater incentive to escape their neighborhoods; thus, the crime rate could be positively associated with enlistment.

Figure 2.23 shows the fraction of high school graduates, age 18 to 40, who are not citizens, by race and ethnicity, from the monthly CPS data. The figure indicates that Hispanics are more likely to be non-citizens, and the fraction has grown from about 0.35 in 1996 to 0.42 in 2007. The fraction has grown for whites and blacks as well, though from a smaller level. For whites, the fraction has grown from 0.015 to 0.024, while for blacks the fraction has grown from 0.039 to 0.057.

Figure 2.24 shows the fraction of the civilian population, age 30 and older, who are veterans, by race and ethnicity. Relative to blacks and Hispanics, whites have the highest proportion of veterans among their 30-and-older population. Between 1996 and 2007, the white veteran population declined from about 20 percent to 15 percent.

Figure 2.23
Fraction of High School Graduates Who Are Noncitizens, by Race/Ethnicity, by Quarter

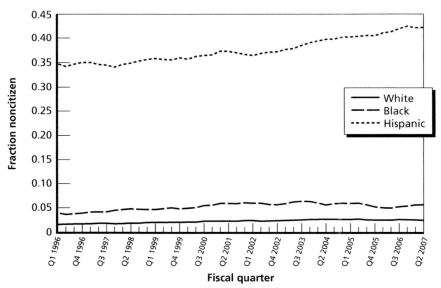

SOURCE: Authors' calculations based on CPS data.
RAND MG861-2.23

Figure 2.24
Fraction of Population, Age 30 and Older, Who Are Veterans, by Race/
Ethnicity, by Quarter

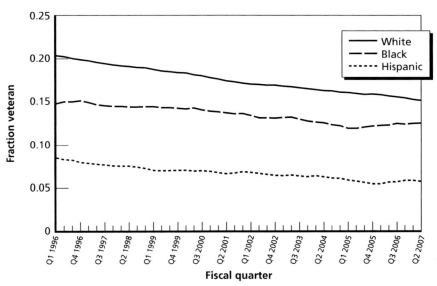

SOURCE: Authors' calculations based on CPS data.
RAND MG861-2.24

The corresponding Hispanic and black veteran populations also declined between 1996 and 2005, but then increased slightly.

Figure 2.25 shows a metric of the crime rate—specifically, the fraction of the population that has been arrested. The FBI Uniform Crime Reports that are the source of the information in Figure 2.25 provide information only for whites and blacks, not Hispanics. The figure shows that the crime rate has declined for blacks, from about 3.3 percent to 2.9 percent between 1998 and 2005.

Figure 2.25
Fraction of Population Arrested, by Race/Ethnicity, by Quarter

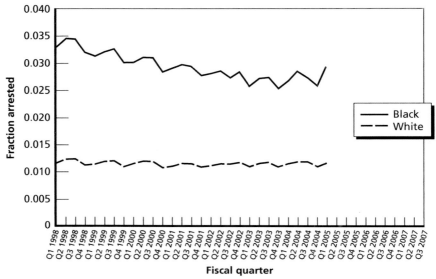

SOURCE: Authors' calculations based on FBI Uniform Crime Reports.
RAND *MG861-2.25*

Political Factors

Simon and Warner (2007) show that high-quality Army enlistments declined during the Iraq war over the period of their data, through 2005. They include a time trend, capturing the Iraq war period, as well as variables representing deaths among all service members and the percentage of a state's population voting for George W. Bush in the 2004 election.

Figure 2.26 shows how support for the president varies by race and ethnicity, as well as by geographic region, in 2005–2006, using data from SurveyUSA. In general, whites age 18 and over indicate greater support for the president than do Hispanics or blacks. Hispanics indicate greater support than do blacks. Among whites, support is higher in the East South Central, West South Central, and Mountain regions. Among Hispanics, support is fairly evenly distributed across

Figure 2.26
Fraction of Population Stating They Support the President, by Race/
Ethnicity, 2005–2006

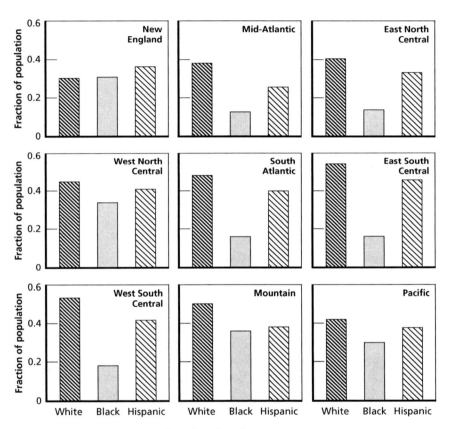

SOURCE: Authors' calculations based on data from SurveyUSA.
NOTES: By census division. Age 18+.
RAND MG861-2.26

regions, except for being somewhat lower in the Mid-Atlantic region.
For blacks, support is also lower in the Mid-Atlantic and South Atlantic
regions as well as in the Central regions (except for West North Central) and is highest in New England, Pacific, and Mountain regions. To
the extent that greater support for the president reflects greater support
for the Iraq war, support for the war is higher among whites.

Summary

High-quality enlistments show distinct trends between the Navy and the Army. While the percentage of contracts that are high-quality fell for the Army, it increased for the Navy, across market segments. Focusing on the trends for blacks, the representation of high-quality enlistments that are black fell dramatically for the Army, whereas black representation was fairly stable for the Navy. For both services, Hispanic representation has increased, though it has been rather stable since mid-2005 for the Army and has continued to increase for the Navy.

Recruiting resources have generally increased in the Army in recent years, in some cases dramatically, such as with bonuses and recruiters. As the Navy contract goal has declined, resources have generally declined too, as in the case of Navy recruiters and the Navy College Fund. Average Navy enlistment bonuses have increased, though. Civilian earnings for high school graduates have been stable for whites and Hispanics and have declined in recent years for blacks. However, military pay has increased.

In terms of demographic trends, the fraction of the high school population that are noncitizens has increased, while the fraction of the 30-and-older population that are veterans has declined, and crime rates have declined among blacks. Support for the Iraq war, as represented by the percentage of the population that indicates support for the president, varies by race and ethnicity, as well as by geographic region.

CHAPTER THREE
Methodology and Data

We are interested in estimating the relationship between high-quality contracts and recruiting resources, on the one hand, and demographic and other factors, on the other. To place our methodology and results into context, we first provide a brief overview of past literature on enlistment supply. Next, we present our methodology and describe the variables we include as well as the data we use. Readers more interested in the policy results can skip the discussion of the methodology in this chapter.

Previous Literature

A substantial literature has been devoted to studying enlistment supply. These studies begin with an economic model of occupational choice, built on the random utility model (McFadden, 1983). At the individual level, an individual, n, chooses to enlist in the military rather than pursue a civilian alternative, j, such as civilian work or college, if enlisting provides greater expected utility relative to the alternatives, or if

$$U_{nm} > U_{nj},$$

where U_{nm} is utility for military service, m, and U_{nj} represents utility for nonmilitary alternatives j for individual n. The probability that individual n chooses the military over the civilian alternative is given as

$$\Pr\left(U_{nm} > U_{nj}\right). \tag{3.1}$$

We can specify the utility of choice k (where k is m or j) as

$$U_{nk} = f_k\left(X_n\right) + \lambda_{nk}, \tag{3.2}$$

where X_n is a set of characteristics of individual n and λ_{nk} is a random error. The characteristics $f_k\left(X_n\right)$ can include such factors as civilian earnings, military earnings, and enlistment bonuses and other factors that affect the individual's decision to enlist, including access to key influencers, such as veterans. The data to estimate an individual enlistment model are individual-level, rather than aggregate, data on individuals choosing the military versus civilian alternatives, such as that gathered via the National Longitudinal Survey of Youth.

This model is a model of the individual's enlistment choice and has been estimated by Hosek and Peterson (1985), Kilburn and Klerman (1999), and Kleykamp (2006) for active duty enlistment, and Arkes and Kilburn (2005) for the reserves. Kilburn and Klerman estimate a multinomial logit model of the decision to enlist, go to college, or pursue other civilian opportunities. They find that the probability of enlistment declines with factors that increase the likelihood of attending college, such as AFQT score and mother's education level, as well as variables that capture the availability of resources to pay for college. In general, in their data from the 1990s, they found that military service and college were substitute activities for high-aptitude youth, while military service and civilian work were substitute activities for other youth. Kleykamp uses data from a survey of recent high school graduates in Texas in 2002. She finds that those with college aspirations are more likely to choose college over military service, but to choose military service over civilian work. She also finds that increases in military presence in a county, measured as the share of county employment that is military, increases the likelihood of choosing the military over other activities.

In this report, we present results of estimation of aggregate enlistment models where the data are not individual-level data but rather data on counts of enlistments in different states over time. The aggregate enlistment model can be derived from the individual occupational choice model as follows. Let U_{nkit} be the utility of individual n, qualified for military service, for alternative k at time t in state i. If P_{it} is the population of qualified individuals in state i at time t, then the expected number of enlistments Y_{it} is given by the size of the population times the probability that an individual in that population would choose the military, or

$$Y_{it} = P_{it} \times \Pr\left(U_{nmit} > U_{njit}\right).$$

Given the definition of U_{nk} for the kth choice in equation 3.2, we get the following:

$$Y_{it} = P_{it} \times \Pr\left(f_m\left(X_n\right) + \lambda_{nm} > f_j\left(X_n\right) + \lambda_{nj}\right)$$
$$= g_{stk}\left(X_n\right) + \lambda_{it}. \qquad (3.3)$$

In words, enlistments in state i at time t depend on the factors that affect the size of the population that is eligible for military service and the factors that affect the occupational choice decision. Among the $g_{stk}\left(X_n\right)$ included in the aggregate model are military pay, civilian pay, recruiting resources (such as bonuses), and factors that affect the size of the eligible population (such the obesity rate). Thus, we are estimating a reduced form model that captures the associations between variables rather than causation.

Warner, Simon, and Payne (2001) and Asch, Hosek, and Warner (2007) review past aggregate enlistment models. Most studies follow the approach developed by Dertouzos (1985), where equation 3.3 is extended to recognize the role of recruiter effort and the military recruiting infrastructure in generating high-quality enlistments. That is, the services do not passively process walk-ins to military recruiting stations but instead actively pursue strategies to increase enlistment supply. These strategies include setting recruiter goals and using incentive plans to reach those goals, to motivate recruiters to focus their effort on high-quality enlistments. The revised model is

$$Y_{it} = g_{stk}\left(X_n\right) + f_{it}\left(R\right) + \lambda_{it}, \qquad (3.4)$$

where $f_{it}\left(R\right)$ captures these "demand-side" factors and depends on the number of recruiters R in a given state at time t. As summarized in Asch, Hosek, and Warner (2007), studies from the 1990s find recruiter elasticities of around 0.5, though Dertouzos and Garber (2003) estimate a recruiter elasticity on the order of around 0.16.[1] In past studies, the elasticity of military pay relative to civilian pay is typically estimated to be around 1.0, and enlistment bonuses are generally estimated to have a relatively small market expansion effect. Bonus elasticities are estimated to be around 0.10. Coefficients on changes in the unemployment rate are generally estimated to be positive but relatively small. Elasticity estimates for the civilian unemployment rate are about 0.20.

Aggregate enlistment models using more recent data, after 2000, are fewer. Simon and Warner (2007) estimate an aggregate enlistment model for the Army using data from a longer period covering 1995 to 2005 as well as a shorter period encompassing 2004 and 2005. For the longer period, they estimate an elasticity of military relative to civilian pay of 0.70 and an elasticity of 1.07 for the shorter period. The unemployment elasticity is 0.42 for the longer period and 0.08 for the shorter period. Thus, changes in the unemployment rate are found to have far smaller effects in more recent years in their study. They estimate that increases in recruiters yield an enlistment elasticity of about 0.48, while decreases in recruiters yield an elasticity estimate of about 0.6. Thus, decreases in the size of the recruiter force have a larger effect than increases. Finally, they estimate the effect on high-quality enlistments of the Iraq war, using three variables: an indicator variable that

---

[1] An elasticity is the percentage increase in high-quality enlistments associated with a 1 percent increase in the factor included in the model. Thus, an elasticity of 0.5 means that a 1 percent increase in recruiters is associated with a 0.5 percent increase in enlistments.

equals 1 during the period of the Iraq war in their data, a variable representing the number of deaths in all four services, and the percentage of the population that voted for George W. Bush in the 2004 election. They find that, during the short period, each year of the Iraq war was associated with a 34 percent decline in Army high-quality enlistments. Casualties had little effect during the short period, but there was relatively little variation in the variable during this period.

Past Studies on the Enlistment Supply of Black and Hispanic Youth

Relatively few studies have focused explicitly on estimating enlistment supply models by race and/or ethnicity. Dale and Gilroy (1984) use aggregate data from 1975 to 1982 and estimate separate aggregate enlistment supply models for whites and blacks. They find that white Army enlistments are responsive to changes in the civilian unemployment rate, but they do not find unemployment effects for black Army enlistments. However, they find both white and black recruits to be responsive to pay and educational benefits.

Kilburn (1992) estimates an individual-level enlistment model by race/ethnicity using the 1979 National Longitudinal Study of Youth. She finds that blacks are more likely to enlist than whites, given eligibility. Hispanics have similar enlistment rates to whites, but are less likely to be eligible to enlist. She finds that blacks are more likely to have characteristics associated with a higher propensity to enlist, such as residence in high-enlistment regions and multiple siblings. She also finds evidence that suggests that, for whites and Hispanics, enlistment rates increase as the difference between military and civilian pay grows. That is, enlistment rates are higher the larger the excess of military over civilian pay. However, she did not find this relationship for blacks. There was little difference in enlistment rates between those with a small excess of military over civilian pay and those with a larger excess. This evidence suggests that blacks are less responsive to changes to military pay relative to civilian pay, compared with whites and Hispanics.

Methodology

We estimate the relationship between high-quality enlistments, Y_{it}, and X_n and R in equation 3.4, using panel regression methods. We emphasize that such regressions measure associations between the variables in the model and do not represent causal effects. In particular, because resources are chosen by policymakers in the services, the Office of the Secretary of Defense (OSD), and Congress based on the conditions prevailing in particular locations and points in time, some of the associations we describe may reflect factors that are unmeasured within the model.

Our empirical approach is similar to that of Warner, Simon, and Payne (2001), and we perform our analysis at the state-quarter level, as a two-way fixed effects model. We partition our covariates into three groups—those that vary both over time and across states (Z_{it}), including X_n and R; those that vary only across states (S_i); and those that vary only over time (T_t). The regression model is

$$Y_{it} = g_{stk}\left(X_n\right) + f_{it}\left(R\right) + \lambda_{it} = \beta_1 Z_{it} + \gamma_i + \theta_t + \varepsilon_{it}, \quad (3.5)$$

where $\lambda_{it} = \gamma_i + \theta_t + \varepsilon_{it}$, γ_i is a vector of state fixed effects, θ_t is a vector of time effects, and ε_{it} is the random effect that captures the omitted variables. It is not possible to identify variables that vary only over time or only across states. Therefore, we estimate the model in two stages. In the first stage, we estimate equation 3.5. In our second stage, we collect the fixed effects γ_i and θ_t, estimated from the first stage, and regress them on S_i and T_t. That is,

$$\hat{\gamma}_i = \beta_2 S_i + \eta_i$$
$$\hat{\theta}_t = \beta_3 T_t + \nu_t. \quad (3.6)$$

Conceptually, the second stage measures how much of the unexplained variation across states and, separately, across time can be explained using the state-varying and time-varying variables in our model.[2] The effects of explanatory variables that vary by both time and location are identified by the comparison of states that experience large changes over time in these variables to states that do not.

This approach has two advantages over more traditional single-step approaches. First, the fixed effects mitigate bias that may arise due to the omission from the model of relevant factors at the state level. For example, the model does not include variables that indicate the quality of the state's university system, which could negatively affect enlistments in a state. The state fixed effects in the model mitigate the omission of such a variable. Second, this approach allows us to estimate the contribution of factors that vary only nationally (such as the wars in Iraq and Afghanistan) or that are fixed over time but vary across states.[3]

To measure the dependent variables—high-quality enlistments in each quarter and state by race and ethnicity and by service—we use data on high-quality gross contracts provided by the U.S. Army and by the U.S. Navy. The data were provided at the level of individual enlistment, and we aggregated the data by state and quarter. Trends in high-quality gross contracts are illustrated in Chapter Two.

Given that services compete for the same pool of high-quality youth, it seems possible that factors chosen by one service might affect enlistments in a competing service. For example, increases in Army recruiters in a particular location might draw recruits who otherwise would have joined the Navy into the Army, in which case Army recruiters would negatively affect Navy enlistments. Although ideally we might wish to allow for the possibility of such cross-service effects in our model, the small sample sizes afforded by an aggregate model (relative

---

[2] Warner, Simon, and Payne (2001) do not separately parcel out state and time fixed effects in the second stage of their model. Although their approach would generate similar coefficient estimates to ours, it complicates the calculation of correct standard errors because their error term exhibits two-way clustering.

[3] Warner, Simon, and Payne (2001) and Plümper and Troeger (2007) provide more in-depth discussions of the two-way fixed effects approach. In a general model, β_2 and β_3 are not identified; the approach essentially identifies these parameters by restricting these coefficients to sum to the state- and time-level means. The obvious drawback is that if the relationships assumed by the restriction are incorrect, the resulting coefficient estimates are inconsistent.

to a model incorporating individual-level data) coupled with the high correlation across services in some incentives, such as bonuses, hamper our ability to precisely estimate such interactions. We instead take the more straightforward route of separately estimating equation 3.5 for each service. Thus, one limitation of our modeling approach is its inability to provide direct evidence regarding cross-service effects.

Variables and Data

Our primary explanatory variables are measures of military recruiting resources—namely, recruiters, enlistment bonuses, college funds, and pay.[4] We measure recruiters relative to the size of the adult population.[5] We measure enlistment bonuses using the average total cash enlistment bonus offered to new recruits in a given state and quarter. We calculate average bonuses from contract microdata provided to us by each of the services.[6] We measure service-level college fund availability as the proportion of new recruits who were offered the college fund.[7]

Because MGIB benefit generosity is determined at the national level, our MGIB measure enters the analysis in the second stage. We measure MGIB benefit generosity using the current maximum annual

---

[4]   Some studies (e.g., Dertouzos and Garber, 2003) consider advertising expenditures as an additional explanatory variable of interest. Some recent research (Dertouzos, 2009) also suggests that groups may vary in their responsiveness to certain types of advertising, such as cable TV commercials. Unfortunately, service-level advertising data of sufficient quality were not available for the entire time period covered by the study, precluding the inclusion of advertising in our analysis. If advertising occurs in areas with positive growth of other resources, our estimates of the effects of these resources may be upwardly biased.

[5]   Navy recruiter data were available only by recruiting district, and some recruiting districts cover areas in multiple states. We developed state-level measures of recruiters by allocating recruiters to states based on the population proportions of the areas covered by each recruiting district.

[6]   Due to a modification of the Army's information technology system in 1999, bonus data are unavailable for the Army during Q2 and Q3 of that year. For these quarters, we impute the average bonus amount over the rest of our sample.

[7]   The actual offer amounts would provide more information than our measure, but college fund amounts were not consistently coded in the microdata.

benefit level at the contract date, and we account for changes in the cost of schooling by denominating this measure using average college tuition.[8] Although measuring the MGIB using contemporaneous benefit levels is not ideal, given that benefits are not actually received until several years later, it seems reasonable to expect that increases in current benefits would affect perceptions of future benefits.[9]

Past researchers have demonstrated that military compensation is highly correlated with enlistments, as discussed earlier in this chapter in our review of past studies. Our pay measure is the ratio of regular military compensation to average civilian pay, where civilian pay has been calculated separately by race/ethnicity using the CPS. Regular military compensation includes basic pay, basic allowance for subsistence, basic allowance for housing, and the tax advantage associated with receiving these allowances tax-free. By constructing our measure as a ratio, we attempt to capture the financial attractiveness of military service relative to other types of employment. Basic pay is set military-wide and does not vary by duty station. Although there is some cross-sectional variation in the military/civilian pay ratio due to differences in average civilian pay across states, this cross-sectional variation is small relative to the variation over time generated by numerous legislative pay raises. We thus enter our pay variable in the second stage of our regression and identify the effects of pay on recruiting using time-series variation.

We also incorporate measures of factors that may affect the eligibility of individuals to enlist, such as obesity or prior involvement in the criminal justice system, since these factors affect the eligibility of minorities differently than that of whites (Asch et al., 2009). Changes

---

[8] We obtained tuition data from the College Board's *Trends in College Pricing* publication series.

[9] Although this measure is appealing for its simplicity, it does not account for the fact that the value of this incentive is ultimately related to expectations for utilization, which may vary for different individuals and are affected by rates of time preference and perceptions of the likely future benefit generosity. An alternative approach for measuring MGIB benefits would be to attempt to predict the likely utilization of benefits based on observable individual characteristics and adjust for the fact that benefits cannot be claimed until the future. In earlier stages of our analysis, we examined this possibility but found that it did not generate substantially different results from the simpler alternative.

in eligibility across market segments will affect enlistment patterns even when all segments are equally responsive to recruiters, bonuses, and other resources under military management. We also attempt to quantify the effects of political factors that may influence enlistment decisions.

The Iraq War

Figures 2.3 and 2.7 in Chapter Two suggest that the invasion and subsequent events in Iraq may have had important effects on military recruiting. Given that the Iraq war was a national policy change, its effects must be identified from the aggregate time series for which there are relatively few degrees of freedom. We correspondingly seek a parsimonious parameterization of the effects of the Iraq war. One possibility is that the initiation of the conflict may have affected recruiting by increasing patriotic sentiment among potential recruits or changing their expectations regarding future deployment. As U.S. involvement in Iraq progressed and news coverage became more negative, the effect of the Iraq war may have become detrimental. We capture these possibilities by allowing an initial level shift in recruiting at the time of the invasion as well as a quadratic time trend in recruiting following the initiation of the Iraq war. A quadratic specification allows the effects of the war to diminish or increase over time for each market segment.[10,11]

Bush Approval Rating

To assess whether the recent enlistment declines are associated with a decrease in support of the president independent of the Iraq war, we also include a measure of public approval of the president. Our public approval measure is an average of responses over a series of 19 surveys conducted in each state by SurveyUSA between May 2005 and

---

[10] Our Iraq war measure may be more properly interpreted as a residual estimated from the aggregate time series that captures attitudes toward military enlistment since the beginning of 2003. Given the dominant role of the war in Iraq in shaping public attitudes toward the military during this period, we find it reasonable to label this an "Iraq war effect." However, this residual may incorporate other factors unrelated to the war.

[11] Using higher-order polynomials yields qualitatively similar conclusions.

November 2006. Unlike better-known national surveys, these survey data provide race-specific measures of approval by state and are available in states with relatively small populations of minorities.[12]

Obesity

Obesity rates among adult Americans rose from 18 percent to 24 percent between 1998 and 2005, and there are substantial differences in obesity rates across market segments. Given that weight is part of the military's medical standard for enlistment, we chose to include a measure of obesity as an additional explanatory factor. We measure obesity using the proportion of the adult population in a state and year that is obese; this variable is taken from the Centers for Disease Control and Prevention's Behavioral Risk Factor Surveillance System and is available separately by race/ethnicity.

Crime Rate

Changes in criminal justice involvement may have affected recent enlistment patterns across segments, both because blacks and Hispanics are arrested at higher rates than other segments and because crime declined substantially between 1998 and 2005. To capture the relationship between changing crime patterns on enlistment, we include the log total number of reported crimes per population in each state and year in our model. Criminal offending data are drawn from the FBI's Uniform Crime Reports.

Noncitizen Share

The U.S. population has experienced appreciable increases in the noncitizen population over the past decade, particularly among Hispanic youth. To capture potential effects of such changes on enlistments, we include the log of the noncitizen proportion of the population by state and year as an additional explanatory variable in our model. The theoretical relationship between citizenship and propensity to enlist is

---

[12] Unfortunately, we were unable to identify surveys with sufficient sample sizes to allow for race-specific approval ratings that varied over time during our sample period, even at the national level.

ambiguous—although noncitizens may be attracted by the expedited naturalization process provided to service members and may have higher levels of patriotism than the general population, the military may present larger language or other assimilation barriers than other types of employment.

Other Modeling Considerations

Rates Versus Counts
Although some research on enlistment supply focuses on enlistment counts, given the substantial size heterogeneity across different states within the United States, we express our variables as population rates or averages to provide for greater comparability across units. Population-weighting the regressions permits us to account for the fact that larger states provide more information about the relative influence of different supply factors.

Logs Versus Levels
Some prior studies estimate enlistment supply models using the raw enlistment rate. In this analysis, we log transform the enlistment rate. For independent variables, log transformation then generates coefficients that are easily interpretable as elasticities and, in some cases, help to correct for a skewed population distribution of the underlying variable. For explanatory variables measuring population proportions (e.g., unemployment rate, veteran status, approval ratings), however, there is no strong reason to prefer logs over levels. For these variables, we choose the transformation that provides the best fit to the data.

Race-Specific Measures
Several of our measures, including presidential approval, obesity, unemployment rates, and college enrollment, were available for both the overall population and specifically by race/ethnicity. Although at first glance it may seem preferable to use race-specific measures when available, disaggregation by race/ethnicity reduces the sample size of these covariates. Doing so may potentially introduce measurement

error. In particular, for variables extracted from the CPS, the small numbers of minorities sampled in some states results in fairly noisy race-specific measures. We attempted to use race-specific demographic measures when feasible.

Data Frequency

Although our analysis incorporates quarterly observations, for a few measures (e.g., population, obesity rate) new data are collected only on an annual basis. For these measures, we use linear interpolation across quarters to smooth changes over time.

Goals

Past research indicates that recruiter effort is an important determinant of recruiting success (Dertouzos, 1985). Insomuch as recruiter effort is correlated with other explanatory variables of interest, failure to control for effort may generate biased estimates of the relationship between high-quality enlistments and resources or other factors. Unfortunately, effort is not directly observable. Following the control function literature (Heckman and Navarro-Lozano, 2004), we attempt to capture the effects of recruiter effort by including recruitment goals as an additional explanatory variable. Here we assume that conditioning on goals removes the dependence between ε_{it} and recruiter effort. Given that effort may vary nonmonotonically with goals, we flexibly model this relationship using a quartic polynomial in goals.

CHAPTER FOUR

Army Results

In this chapter, we discuss the results of the estimation of the Army enlistment models by market segment, use them to decompose the recent trends in black and Hispanic representation in terms of exploratory variables, and provide marginal cost estimates. Our key result is that the decline in black representation among high-quality enlistments in the Army appears to be primarily due to (1) the larger negative effects of the Iraq war on black enlistments than on the enlistments of Hispanics and whites and (2) the success of the Army in enlisting Hispanics and whites as a result of pay and educational benefits. The Army's success with the latter two groups resulted in an increase in the share of whites and Hispanics among high-quality enlistments but a decline in the share of black enlistments. As discussed in Chapter Three, our regression analysis measures associations between the variables in the model and does not represent causal effects. Some of the associations we describe may reflect factors that are unmeasured within the model.

Estimated Effects from the Army Model

Table 4.1 reports coefficients from regression estimates with heteroskedasticity-robust standard errors clustered at the state level. We illustrate the results graphically and compare the results across market segments.

Table 4.1
Coefficient Estimates of Army Enlistment Supply Models, by Market
Segment, Dependent Variable = Log(High-Quality Enlistments/Population)

Explanatory Variable	Black	White	Hispanic
Log(bonus amount)	0.201**	0.155**	0.134
	(0.0534)	(0.0284)	(0.0944)
Log(recruiters/population)	0.619**	0.512**	0.788**
	(0.0845)	(0.0597)	(0.121)
Log(military/civilian pay)	0.523	1.82**	2.35*
	(0.745)	(0.653)	(1.16)
Log(MGIB benefit/tuition)	0.377	0.312	0.744
	(0.333)	(0.282)	(0.518)
Percentage receiving Army College Fund	−0.138	0.117	0.832*
	(0.442)	(0.169)	(0.381)
Iraq war effect	−0.598**	−0.241**	−0.242†
	(0.101)	(0.0833)	(0.127)
Bush approval rating	0.192	0.128	−0.585**
	(0.172)	(0.134)	(0.155)
Log(unemployment rate)	0.0160	0.0500**	−0.00190
	(0.0218)	(0.0163)	(0.0246)
Log(% veteran)	0.150	0.217	1.08**
	(0.238)	(0.177)	(0.405)
Log(% noncitizen)	−0.0689†	0.0442*	0.123
	(0.0365)	(0.0217)	(0.0835)
Log(% obese)	−0.117	−0.229†	0.165
	(0.0979)	(0.117)	(0.108)
Percentage enrolled in college	0.00401	−0.332†	0.226
	(0.244)	(0.200)	(0.341)

Table 4.1—Continued

Explanatory Variable	Black	White	Hispanic
Log(crime rate)	0.586**	0.371*	−0.0762
	(0.223)	(0.165)	(0.362)
N	1,653	1,899	1,638

NOTES: The table reports coefficient estimates from a regression relating the log number of high-quality enlistments per population to factors affecting enlistment supply. The regression is estimated using a two-stage approach described in Chapter Three; the first stage incorporates year and state fixed effects. The unit of observation is a state and quarter; the sample includes the 50 U.S. states during the period between Q1 1998 and Q2 2007. Standard errors clustered on state are reported in parentheses.

† Denotes statistical significance at the 10 percent level.

* Denotes statistical significance at the 5 percent level.

** Denotes statistical significance at the 1 percent level.

Effects of Recruiting Resources

Potential recruits have traditionally been thought to be highly responsive to changes in military pay. Warner, Simon, and Payne (2001) estimate a pay elasticity of 1.05 for the Army, roughly twice their estimated recruiter elasticity, while Bohn and Schmitz (1996) estimate a Navy pay elasticity of 1.64. In our sample, estimated pay elasticities for whites and Hispanics are even larger, at 1.82 and 2.35, respectively. Thus, a 10 percent increase in the military/civilian pay ratio increases high-quality Army contracts for whites and Hispanics by 18.2 percent and 23.5 percent, respectively, as shown in Figure 4.1. For blacks, the pay elasticity is less than one-third that of other segments and is not statistically different from zero. Figure 4.1 shows the estimated change in high-quality enlistments as a result of a 10 percent change in the military pay relative to civilian pay. The black whisker shows the confidence interval of the estimate, given the standard error estimates in Table 4.1. If the confidence interval includes zero, i.e., the black whisker crosses the x-axis in Figure 4.1, then the estimated effect is not statistically different from zero.

Examining the time-series patterns in enlistments and pay from Figures 2.4–2.6 and 2.15 provides insights into the pay elasticity esti-

Figure 4.1
Estimated Percentage Change in Army High-Quality Enlistments Due to a
10 Percent Change in the Ratio of Military to Civilian Pay

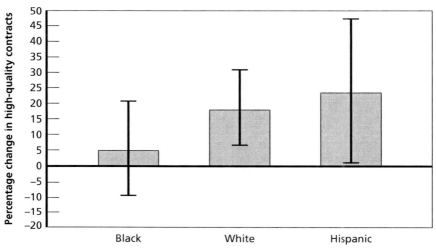

mates shown in Figure 4.1. The large pay increase after 2000 was followed by substantial growth in both Hispanic and white enlistments over the next two years. Black enlistments remained stable or slightly declined. Apparently blacks did not respond to large changes in military compensation, an intuition that is formalized by the pay elasticities in Figure 4.1.

To give context to these estimates, during this period, relative military pay rose by 23.6 percent for blacks, 28.9 percent for whites, and 18 percent for Hispanics. Our estimated elasticities indicate that pay increases can account for 12.4 percent, 52.6 percent, and 41.3 percent of the growth in black, white, and Hispanic high-quality Army contracts over this period. The percentage change for black enlistments is not statistically different from zero.

All market segments are highly responsive to recruiters, with estimated elasticities ranging between 0.5 and 0.8. The estimates are similar to those reported in Murray and McDonald (1999); Warner, Simon, and Payne (2001); and Simon and Warner (2007). Thus, as shown in Figure 4.2, a 10 percent increase in recruiters implies a 6.2 percent, 5.1 percent, and 7.9 percent increase in Army high-quality enlistments for blacks, whites, and Hispanics, respectively. The largest changes in the number of recruiters occurred from 2004 through 2006, with overall increases of 21.4 percent. Given our estimates, the increase in recruiters alone can explain growth of 11 to 17 percent in high-quality enlistments during this period.

For enlistment bonuses, in contrast, the point estimate for blacks is 50 percent higher than that for Hispanics and suggests a 2.0 percent increase in black high-quality contracts associated with each 10 percent increase in the average bonus amount (see Figure 4.3). For whites and blacks, the implied increase is smaller, at 1.5 percent and 1.3 percent, respectively. However, the Army increased the average enlistment bonus dramatically during our sample, more than doubling average bonuses between 2000 and 2006. Therefore, although the absolute effects of bonuses are modest, because bonuses grew so much during

Figure 4.2
Estimated Percentage Change in Army High-Quality Enlistments Due to a 10 Percent Change in Production Recruiters

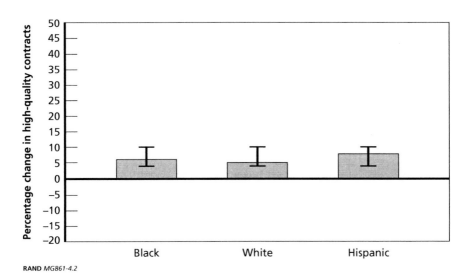

RAND *MG861-4.2*

Figure 4.3
Estimated Percentage Change in Army High-Quality Enlistments Due to a
10 Percent Change in Mean Enlistment Bonus Amount

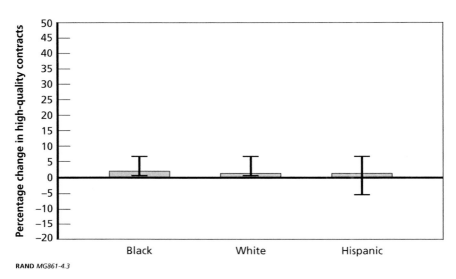

our sample period, bonuses can explain growth of 20–30 percent in high-quality contracts.

Turning to educational benefits, we find that only Hispanics display evidence of responsiveness to these benefits, with large estimated elasticities for both the MGIB and the Army College Fund. For Hispanics, extending Army College Fund eligibility to an additional 10 percent of incoming high-quality recruits is associated with an 8 percent increase in Hispanic recruits, as shown in Figure 4.4. Point estimates for all market segments are positive for the MGIB, although the fairly wide standard errors for these estimates make it difficult to exclude effects of meaningful magnitude. Substantial collinearity between the MGIB, pay, and Iraq war measures account for some of this imprecision. Additionally, it may be the case that improved outside scholarship opportunities and a better civilian labor market have made college funds less relevant in the enlistment decision process for blacks.

Figure 4.4
Estimated Percentage Change in Army High-Quality Enlistments Due to a
10 Percent Change in Army College Fund Eligibility

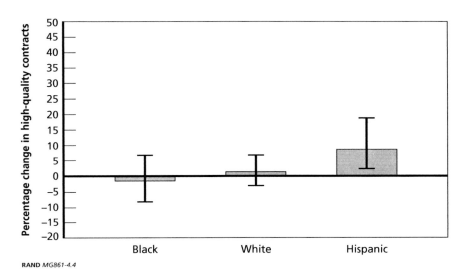

RAND MG861-4.4

Effects of the Iraq War

We find important differences across market segments in the estimated effects of the Iraq war. Averaging across the post-invasion period, our estimates imply a 45 percent drop in black enlistments compared with a 21 percent drop for white and Hispanics. As discussed below, this differential responsiveness to operations in Iraq has important implications for black representation in the Army. The counterintuitive negative coefficient on presidential approval for Hispanics is driven almost entirely by the state of New York, which had high enlistment rates but very low presidential approval.

Whereas the average "Iraq effect" over the post-invasion period is negative, Figure 4.5 plots the quadratic time trends implied by our estimated coefficients by race/ethnicity. For whites and Hispanics, the initial effects of the invasion appear positive, but the effect is negative for all segments by mid-2004. By the end of the sample, the estimated Iraq effects appear surprisingly large. Figure 2.7 and Figures 2.11 through 2.16 help to explain this finding. Figures 2.11 through 2.16 show that,

Figure 4.5
Estimated Effects of the Iraq War for the Army, by Market Segment

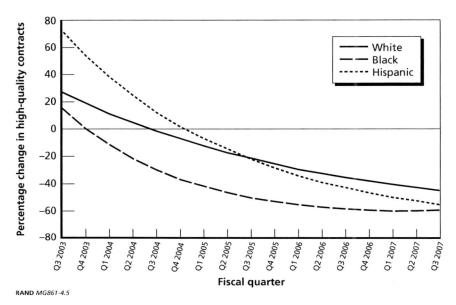

RAND *MG861-4.5*

between mid-2004 and 2007, the Army substantially increased highly effective recruiting resources, including increasing its recruiter force by about a third and tripling average enlistment bonuses. Furthermore, regular military compensation increased by 10 percent. However, Figure 2.7 indicates that contract counts per 100,000 remained relatively stagnant over this period. Our model estimates large negative Iraq residuals to reconcile these two observations. In other words, the stagnation in contracts despite the increase in resources is attributed to the Iraq war, holding other factors constant.

Interestingly, the basic patterns in Figure 4.5 suggest that, although the effects of Iraq were more highly negative and more rapidly felt among blacks, they had largely played out among this segment by 2006. For whites and Hispanics, in contrast, the data suggest that the deleterious effects of the war continue to expand.

Our results regarding the differential effects of the Iraq war by market segment are consistent with survey evidence that demonstrates sharply differing attitudes toward the war across market segments.

Table 4.2 analyzes pooled data from two ABC News/*Washington Post* polls, conducted in April 2005 and June 2006, in which a nationally representative group of respondents were questioned regarding their attitudes toward the Iraq war and military service. Column 1 reports coefficient estimates from a regression in which the dependent variable is a 0/1 variable indicating that the respondent believed that the war in Iraq was worth it and the explanatory variables are indicators for the race of the respondent. These regressions also control for respondent age, gender, income, and educational attainment. The coefficient of −0.30 for blacks indicates that blacks were 30 percentage points less likely than whites to believe that the Iraq war was worth fighting. Hispanics were also less supportive of the war than whites, although they were more supportive than blacks. These differences across groups are highly statistically significant.

Column 2 reports results of a regression in which the dependent variable is a 0/1 indicator for whether an individual would recommend military service to a young person. Controlling for demographic characteristics, blacks were about 50 percent less likely to recommend military service than whites, while Hispanics were about 25 percent less likely to recommend military service than whites. The final column of Table 4.2 replicates this regression but adds indicators for attitudes regarding the war in Iraq as additional explanatory variables. The omitted group is those who strongly agree that the war was worth fighting. These individual attitudinal variables are highly statistically significant, and they more strongly predict support for military service than any of the other demographic characteristics included in the model. Additionally, after controlling for attitudes toward the Iraq war, the coefficients for blacks become substantially smaller, while the coefficients for Hispanics become insignificantly different from zero. Thus, much of the differences across groups in the willingness to recommend military service can be explained by differences in attitudes regarding the Iraq war.

These survey results indicate that, by 2005, blacks were less positively disposed toward military service than other groups and that this disfavor was linked to negative attitudes regarding the Iraq war. This finding is consistent with the pattern revealed by our aggregate enlistment model, which indicated that high-quality enlistments among

Table 4.2
Regression Estimates of Differences in Attitudes Toward the Iraq War and Military Service, by Market Segment

Dependent Variable	1 Believe Iraq War Worth It	2 Would Recommend Military Service	3 Would Recommend Military Service
Mean	0.549	0.461	0.461
Explanatory Variable			
Race (Omitted Group: White)			
Black	−0.308**	−0.247**	−0.104*
	(0.035)	(0.041)	(0.052)
Hispanic	−0.194**	−0.120*	−0.019
	(0.049)	(0.054)	(0.059)
Believe Iraq War Worth It (Omitted Group: Strongly Agree)			
Somewhat agree			−0.264**
			(0.036)
Somewhat disagree			−0.427**
			(0.026)
Somewhat disagree			−0.569**
			(0.024)
N	1,700	1,663	1,647
Control for age, education, and income?	Yes	Yes	Yes

SOURCE: Author calculations based on data from the April 2005 and June 2006 ABC News/*Washington Post* monthly polls.

NOTES: Estimation was accomplished using probit regression; reported coefficients are marginal effects evaluated at the means of the independent variables. Heteroskedasticity-robust standard errors are reported in parentheses.

* Denotes statistical significance at the 5 percent level.

** Denotes statistical significance at the 1 percent level.

blacks were more adversely affected by the Iraq war than white or Hispanic enlistments.

Effects of the Unemployment Rate and Demographic Variables

Our coefficient estimates on the unemployment rate and on demographic variables provide a mixed portrait of the role of demographic and economic factors in explaining recent Army high-quality enlistments (see Figures 4.6 through 4.10). Coefficients are most precisely estimated among whites, for whom unemployment and noncitizen share are positively and significantly associated with enlistments. However, the magnitude of the unemployment coefficients is small, indicating, for example, that a doubling of the unemployment rate would generate an increase in high-quality white enlistment of only 5 percent (as shown in Figure 4.6). The rising obesity rate reduces the population that is eligible for enlistment and has a negative effect on enlistment supply (see Figure 4.7). For whites, the 35 percent increase in the adult obesity rate between 1998 and 2007 is estimated to be associated with an 8 percent decline in white high-quality enlistments. For blacks and Hispanics, the role of demographic factors is less apparent, given the imprecision of many of our coefficient estimates. Interestingly, the association between veteran share and enlistments is much stronger for

Figure 4.6
Estimated Percentage Change in Army High-Quality Enlistments Due to a 10 Percent Change in the Civilian Unemployment Rate

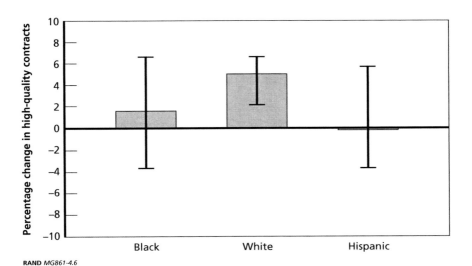

RAND MG861-4.6

Figure 4.7
**Estimated Percentage Change in Army High-Quality Enlistments Due to a
10 Percent Change in the Civilian Adult Obesity Rate**

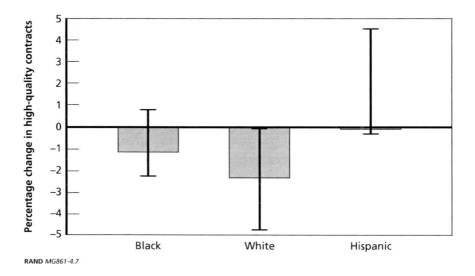

Figure 4.8
**Estimated Percentage Change in Army High-Quality Enlistments Due to a
10 Percent Change in the Size of the Veterans' Population**

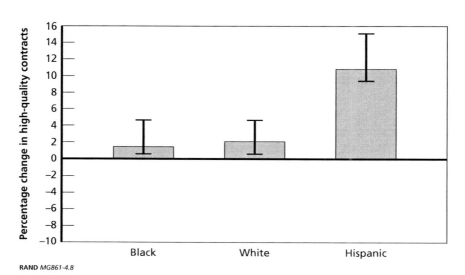

Figure 4.9
Estimated Percentage Change in Army High-Quality Enlistments Due to a
10 Percent Change in the Size of the Crime Rate

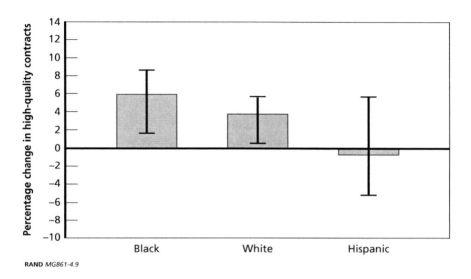

Figure 4.10
Estimated Percentage Change in Army High-Quality Enlistments Due to a
10 Percent Change in the Percentage of the Population That Is Noncitizen

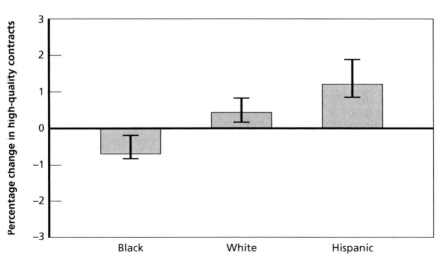

Hispanics than other segments, as shown in Figure 4.8. The change in the veteran share of the population between 1998 and 2007 is associated with a 28 percent decline in the supply of high-quality Hispanic enlistments and a 6 percent decline in the supply of high-quality white enlistments.

If crime rates affect enlistments primarily by reducing the pool of eligible youth, we might expect negative coefficients on crime rates (Figure 4.9). Our estimates are positive and significant for blacks and whites, however, suggesting that a different mechanism is at work. Given that we focus on high-quality youth, for whom criminal participation is relatively infrequent, our findings are perhaps unsurprising. One interpretation of our estimates is that military service becomes more attractive than other opportunities in areas experiencing increases in social problems, such as crime. However, there are many other potential explanations for this finding.

The noncitizen share of the adult population grew from 9.8 percent to 13.3 percent between 1998 and 2007, an increase of roughly a third (Figure 4.10). Interestingly, our estimates indicate that growth in the noncitizen population is associated with declines in black enlistments and increases in white enlistments. Immigration can explain a modest decline of 2.4 percent in black enlistments during the sample period and an increase of 1.5 percent in white enlistments. As one might expect, the strongest effect of immigration is present among Hispanics, whose high-quality enlistments increased by an estimated 4.3 percent as a result of immigration, although this relationship is only marginally statistically significant.

Effects of Goals

Our approach of modeling the effects of goals flexibly using a polynomial permits us to calculate the association between goals and enlistments at varying goal levels and allows for the possibility of a nonlinear relationship between these factors. Such nonlinearities seem intuitively plausible. For example, goals established below enlistment levels that can be readily achieved with minimal effort are likely to elicit little response by recruiters. Similarly, recruiters may fail to respond to goals set at unrealistically high levels, since goal achievement in these contexts would be unlikely even with large expenditures of effort.

Figure 4.11 plots the estimated effects of a unit increase in the contract goal on white, black, and Hispanic high-quality enlistments. The x-axis ranges over values observed in the data; the average Army goal over our sample period is 130 contracts per 100,000 in the population. The figure demonstrates, for example, that an increase in the goal from 130 to 131 contracts per 100,000 is associated with an increase in high-quality contracts of 0.67 percent for Hispanics, 0.21 percent for blacks, and 0.14 percent for whites. Thus, at average goal levels, increases in goals are linked with augmented minority representation.

Two other notable patterns emerge from the figure. Goal changes at the lowest goal levels are not associated with increases in enlistments, a pattern consistent with the notion that goals that are "too easy" do not elicit additional recruiter effort.[1] Additionally,

Figure 4.11
Estimated Percentage Change in High-Quality Army Enlistments Associated with a Unit Change in Goals, at Varying Goal Levels

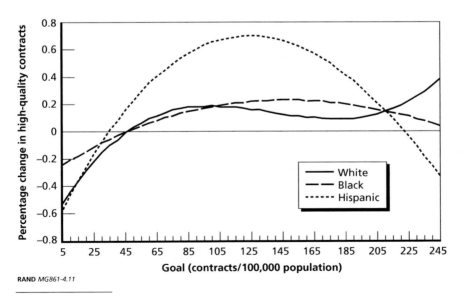

RAND MG861-4.11

---

[1] This pattern would also be consistent with a situation in which areas that experience large negative shocks to recruiting also decrease goals.

at the highest observed goal levels, estimated changes for whites lie above those for blacks and Hispanics, suggesting that recruiters may focus attention away from minorities at particularly high goal levels.

Accounting for Recent Changes in Minority Representation

The estimates presented in Table 4.1 and illustrated in Figures 4.1 through 4.11 indicate differential responsiveness of market segments to several key resource measures. An important question is the extent to which each explanatory factor contributed to the trends apparent in Figure 2.4. For example, the figure indicates that, between Q4 2000 and Q4 2004, the black share of new enlistments dropped from 18.9 percent to 10.6 percent, a difference of 8.3 percentage points.

To decompose this 8.3 percentage point national change, for each explanatory factor, we use the coefficient estimates reported in Table 4.1 to recalculate expected enlistments under the assumption that this factor had remained constant at its Q4 2000 level through Q4 2004. By comparing the expected enlistments with actual enlistments, we are able to estimate the contribution of that factor to the overall Q4 2000–Q4 2004 changes. We report the results of this decomposition in Tables 4.3 (for 2000–2004) and 4.4 (for 2005–2007).

Because the outcomes of interest in the two tables are high-quality recruit representation or shares, the relative responsiveness of different market segments to each incentive, rather than the absolute magnitude of the responsiveness of each market segment, determines whether the share rises or falls with a given factor. Thus, if enlistments for whites, blacks, and Hispanics increase when a given factor increases (say, military pay), but enlistments for one segment (say, blacks) increase less than for the other segments, then that segment's share of high-quality enlistments will decline.

Furthermore, the magnitude and direction of changes in the underlying explanatory variable of interest are also critical in determining whether the shares of high-quality enlistments rise or fall. For example, the average number of Army recruiters fell between Q4 2000 and Q4 2004, so the market segment that is the most responsive to recruiters, namely blacks, experienced a resulting drop in share.

As shown in Table 4.3, the decomposition indicates that most of the decline in black representation between Q4 2000 and Q4 2004 can be explained by the Iraq war and changes in military pay. Of the 8.3 percentage point drop, 5.2 percentage points, or 63 percent of the total, can be attributed to differential responsiveness of market segments to the Iraq war. Whereas the Iraq effect represents an erosion of support for enlistment among blacks, the pay effect actually reflects a sort of recruiting success. Because of the enormous improvements in the recruitment of whites and Hispanics following the 2001 pay increase, blacks, who were relatively less responsive to pay, lost share.

Figure 2.4 indicates that, after a steady five-year decline, black share recovered somewhat between Q4 2005 and Q3 2007, gaining 2.1 percentage points. Table 4.4 performs a similar decomposition of changes in black share over this period. The model is somewhat less successful at explaining these recent trends, predicting only a 1.3 percentage point increase in black share over this period. Military pay and the Iraq war are again the most important factors driving the change. Although the sign on the effect of the Iraq war seems counterintuitive at first, Figure 4.5 provides an explanation for this seeming incongruity. Because the effects of the Iraq war had largely stabilized for blacks by this period but were continuing to increase for white and Hispanics, the war actually shifted representation in favor of blacks. This increase was partly offset by declines in black representation due to increases in military pay.[2]

Table 4.5 shows a similar decomposition for the increase in Hispanic high-quality representation, focusing on the period between Q1 2000 and Q4 2003. After rising only 1 percentage point in the previous three years, Hispanic share increased by 3.3 percentage points between the beginning of 2000 and the end of 2003. Unsurprisingly, our decomposition attributes a large portion (25 percent) of this increase to the

---

[2] Because our model ultimately captures the Iraq effect using a time-series residual, it is possible that other unobserved factors that varied over time and across market segments can explain the changes in Table 4.4. For example, a subtle change in Army recruiting behavior to focus on blacks after 2005 could also explain some of what we label to be an effect of the Iraq war.

Table 4.3
Decomposition of Black High-Quality Representation Between 2000 and 2004

Explanatory Factor	Explained Change (%)
Bonuses	0.3
Recruiters	−0.3
Relative military pay	−2.0
MGIB	0.0
Army College Fund	0.2
Iraq war	−5.2
Other	−1.0
Total change predicted by model	−8.0
Total actual change	−8.3
Unexplained	−0.3

Table 4.4
Decomposition of Black High-Quality Representation Between 2005 and 2007

Explanatory Factor	Explained Change (%)
Enlistment bonuses	0.0
Production recruiters	−0.1
Relative military pay	−1.2
MGIB	−0.1
Army College Fund	0.0
Iraq war	2.3
Other	0.5
Total change predicted by model	1.3
Total actual change	2.1
Unexplained	0.8

Table 4.5
Decomposition of Hispanic High-Quality Representation Between 2000 and 2003

Explanatory Factor	Explained Change (%)
Enlistment bonuses	0.1
Production recruiters	0.2
Relative military pay	0.6
MGIB	1.4
Army College Fund	0.0
Iraq war	0.0
Other	0.3
Total change predicted by model	2.5
Total actual change	3.3
Unexplained	0.8

2001 pay enhancements, although college funds contribute an additional 56 percent. The acceleration in Hispanic enlistments occurred during a period of substantial increase in MGIB benefits.

Cost Calculations

Given our findings that individuals from different market segments exhibit different levels of responsiveness to incentives, a natural question is how the cost of recruiting individuals varies by recruiting resource and segment. Because recruiting resources generally do not target individuals by race/ethnicity, varying the amount of a resource simultaneously affects recruiting yields for all types of enlistments. Thus, calculating the marginal cost of a recruit from a particular market segment is problematic. More appropriately interpreted, our cost estimates characterize how recruiting resources vary in both their cost per recruit generated as well as types of enlistments they generate.

Table 4.6 reports the numbers of high-quality enlistments associated with an additional $1 million in spending by market segment. To calculate the values in the table, we compute the percentage change in each incentive associated with a $1 million expenditure increase and multiply this by the percentage change in enlistments implied by our elasticity estimates. For example, a $1 million increase in bonuses expands bonus availability by 0.55 percent (1/180), an increase that would augment black high-quality enlistments by 0.11 percent based on our elasticity estimate for blacks of 0.20. Given that there are roughly 6,500 such enlistments in the Army each year, this translates to an additional seven high-quality black enlistments. Market segment differences in predicted enlistment levels thus represent both differences in responsiveness by market segment to each incentive and differences in the base enlistment rates. For example, because there are roughly 30,000 high-quality white enlistments each year but 6,500 black enlistments, a 1 percent change for each market segment would

Table 4.6
Army Marginal Cost Estimates: Total New High-Quality Enlistments Associated with $1 Million Additional Spending on Incentives

	Enlistment Bonus	Recruiters	Regular Military Compensation	Army College Fund
White	27	23	35	11
Black	7	6	2	0
Hispanic	3	5	6	10
Total high-quality recruits	37	34	43	21
A. Cost per recruit ($)[a]	27,000	22,900	26,300	47,600
B. Cost per recruit ($)[b]	34,400	29,400		

[a] Enlistment bonus figure based on an expenditure of $180 million; recruiter figure based on cost per recruiter of $100,000.

[b] Enlistment bonus figure based on an expenditure of $238 million; recruiter figure based on cost per recruiter of $130,000.

generate a substantially higher number of white enlistees than black enlistees.

Table 4.6 presents two marginal cost estimates (labeled "A" and "B") to illustrate the sensitivity of the estimates to budget outlays. There is substantial variation in the total outlays associated with various recruiting incentives during the years of our data. Accounting data provided to RAND by the OSD indicate that the Army spent an average of $500 million annually for recruiter compensation (about $92,000 per recruiter) and $240 million each year for recruiter support activities ($40,000 per recruiter) between 2000 and 2007, or approximately $130,000 per recruiter. We use this estimate of $130,000 per recruiter for the marginal cost calculations labeled "B" in Table 4.6. However, military pay increases and a challenging recruiting environment have substantially increased the cost of recruiters in recent years. For example, Warner, Simon, and Payne (2001) used a per-recruiter cost of only $55,000, including only $11,000 in support costs. We therefore also consider a lower estimate of $100,000 per recruiter to compute marginal cost in Table 4.6 (labeled "A").

Between 2000 and 2007, the Army spent an additional $180 million per year on enlistment bonuses, or $4,200 per high-quality recruit. As shown in Figure 2.13, average bonuses increased in the Army. The Army's enlistment bonus budget increased as well, from $106 million (in 2006 dollars) in 2000 to $238 million in 2007. We compute the marginal cost assuming a budget of $180 million ("A") and $238 million ("B") in Table 4.6. As shown in the table, the marginal cost estimate increases at higher budget outlays for bonuses.

Military pay increased as well. Regular military compensation for new enlistments accounted for an additional $1.9 billion in annual expenditures in 2006 dollars.[3] The average regular military compensa-

---

[3]   Given the structure of military pay, it would be difficult to increase military pay for new recruits without a corresponding increase for all service members. At the same time, using the total cost of a military-wide pay increase in our calculations would be inappropriate, since such pay increases generate additional effects beyond increases in enlistments. As a compromise and following the approach of Warner, Simon, and Payne (2001), we use the cost of pay increases for all entering service members' first year as our measure of the cost of changes in military pay. This is clearly an underestimate of the total cost of pay increases.

tion cost of a new recruit in the first year is $27,400 in 2006 dollars. Given that the military must raise the pay of all recruits, not just high-quality ones, when it uses pay to expand the market, we compute the marginal cost of pay, given our elasticity estimates, as $26,300.

Additional annual expenditures by the Army for the Army College Fund averaged $47.2 million. These expenditures are the amount the Army must pay the Treasury and represent the actuarial value of the expected benefit times the number of Army College Fund offers. The computation of the actuarial value recognizes that not all members who take the Army College Fund offer will complete the minimum service required to receive the benefit, attend an eligible institution, and use all of the benefit. Given our elasticity estimates, the marginal cost of the Army College Fund is $47,600. The marginal cost is relatively high because $1 million additional spending produces only 21 recruits, fewer than pay, recruiters, or enlistment bonuses. One reason the program produces relatively few recruits is that the Army offers the program to relatively few high-quality recruits, about 14 percent on average, as shown in Figure 2.16.

Two points are noteworthy in Table 4.6. First, consider the marginal cost figures. Recruiters are relatively more cost-effective, when recruiters are lower-cost (at $100,000 per recruiter), but, as cost per recruiter rises to $130,000, the cost advantage of recruiters disappears. Specifically, under assumption "A," the marginal cost of recruiters is $22,900 but increases to $29,400 when the average cost of a recruiter increases. As enlistment bonus budgets have increased, the marginal cost of bonuses has increased as well. At higher budgets, the marginal cost of enlistment bonuses is estimated at $34,400. Table 4.6 indicates that the Army College Fund is no longer among the most cost-effective recruiting resources, as found in past research (Warner, Simon, and Payne, 2001). The Army College Fund is offered to relatively few enlistments, but its actuarial cost has increased, per taker, likely because the probability of using the benefit increases as the value of the benefit increases.

A second key point in Table 4.6 is that the same expenditure of resources, $1 million, does not always produce the same composition of enlistments in terms of market segmentation. Enlistment bonuses and recruiters generate a similar composition of high-quality enlistments by race/ethnicity, producing a recruit force that is roughly 20 percent black and has a smaller proportion of Hispanics. Military pay generates a less diverse set of high-quality enlistments. About 80 percent (or 35) of the 43 new enlistments are white, 14 percent are Hispanic, and about 5 percent are black. The low responsiveness of blacks to the Army College Fund makes this incentive less attractive in terms of recruiting a larger share of blacks but more attractive in terms of recruiting a larger share of Hispanics.

In interpreting these estimates, it is important to recognize that we focus on high-quality recruiting as our outcome, and not on other outcomes of interest. For example, enlistment bonuses are used to channel enlistments into hard-to-fill occupations, and they may be cost-effective as a skill-channeling resource rather than as a market expander. There are other limitations to the cost analysis that argue for caution in interpreting the marginal cost estimates. Cost calculations implicitly assume that the measured relationships represent causal effects and do not reflect unobserved factors excluded from the model. In the presence of such misspecification, the cost estimates may not correctly portray the consequences of additional investments in a particular resource.[4] For some resources, such as pay for blacks, however, our model estimates are sufficiently imprecise that the true effect of an additional investment may be appreciably different from the effect we report based on our point estimate. Finally, our cost calculations assume that increased expenditures lead to proportional increases in the actual amount of effective resources.[5] Although the specific cost estimates in Table 4.6 are likely inexact given these limitations, overall, it appears that bonuses, recruiters, and pay are roughly comparable in their cost-effectiveness, and it appears that similar types of resource

---

[4] We substitute zero values for point estimates, which are negative but not statistically significantly different from zero under the assumption that additional incentives are unlikely to discourage people from joining.

[5] This is akin to assuming a constant return technology for generating production resources, in which case average costs are equivalent to marginal costs.

expenditures can produce different outcomes in terms of the diversity of high-quality enlistments.

Summary

Our empirical estimates for the Army indicate several differences across market segments in responsiveness to resource and demographic changes. We find that whites and Hispanics are more responsive to changes in relative military pay than blacks, while blacks respond more to recruiters and bonuses. Recruiters are productive across all market segments, while Hispanics appear most responsive to educational benefits. Relative to resources and the Iraq war, demographic changes appear less able to explain the recent trends in enlistments, although, in some cases, we find statistically significant relationships between these factors and high-quality enlistments.

In considering the shifts in minority representation that initially motivated our analysis, we find a dual explanation for the decline in black share among high-quality enlistees. Initial declines in this share appear to reflect the success of recruiting among other market segments, particularly following the large basic pay increase of 2001. Later erosion in black share appears attributable to the Iraq war, which negatively affected all market segments but had a particularly acute effect among blacks. Growth in Hispanic share seems largely related to increases in pay and college benefits.

CHAPTER FIVE

Navy Results

In this chapter, we discuss the Navy results and use the parameter estimates to explain the factors affecting changes in the representation of blacks and Hispanics in recent years and to estimate marginal costs. In general, we find smaller differences across market segment in the effects of recruiting resources than we observed in the Army. Furthermore, the effects of the Iraq war on high-quality enlistment supply are positive for blacks and Hispanics, unlike the effects we find for the Army.

Estimated Effects from the Navy Model

The parameter estimates and standard errors of our Navy model are presented in Table 5.1 for each market segment.

Effects of Recruiting Resources

The effects of military pay relative to civilian pay, production recruiters, and average enlistment bonus on high-quality Navy contracts are shown in Figures 5.1 through 5.3. The military pay elasticity ranges from 0.3 to 2.3. Only the pay effect for white enlistments is estimated with precision, and this effect is relatively large, implying a 25 percent increase in white high-quality enlistments for a 10 percent increase in the military/civilian pay ratio.

The results for production recruiters and Navy enlistment bonuses suggest relatively little variation across market segments in the association between high-quality Navy enlistments and these resources. For example, a 10 percent increase in Navy recruiters is associated with a

Table 5.1
Coefficient Estimates of Navy Enlistment Supply Models, by Market Segment, Dependent Variable = Log(High-Quality Enlistments/Population)

Explanatory Variable	Black	White	Hispanic
Log(bonus amount)	−0.0674	0.0527*	0.0897
	(0.0723)	(0.0225)	(0.113)
Log(recruiters/population)	0.528**	0.518**	0.556**
	(0.153)	(0.0580)	(0.185)
Log(military/civilian pay)	0.769	2.27**	0.294
	(0.706)	(0.510)	(0.363)
Log(MGIB benefit/tuition)	−0.350	−0.554*	−0.164
	(0.325)	(0.239)	(0.228)
Percentage receiving Navy College Fund	0.0978	0.0521	−0.268
	(0.326)	(0.118)	(0.434)
Iraq war effect	0.0721	−0.185**	0.219**
	(0.0863)	(0.0637)	(0.0472)
Bush approval rating	0.137	0.134	−0.580†
	(0.101)	(0.137)	(0.299)
Log(unemployment rate)	0.00193	0.0250**	0.0251
	(0.0211)	(0.00951)	(0.0278)
Log(% veteran)	−0.0618	−0.263*	0.467
	(0.305)	(0.117)	(0.586)
Log(% noncitizen)	0.0158	0.0106	0.410**
	(0.0400)	(0.0176)	(0.124)
Log(% obese)	−0.132	−0.0918	0.0839
	(0.107)	(0.105)	(0.126)
Percentage enrolled in college	−0.0312	−0.0623	0.317
	(0.305)	(0.238)	(0.437)

Table 5.1—Continued

Explanatory Variable	Black	White	Hispanic
Log(crime rate)	0.182	0.204	0.937
	(0.356)	(0.143)	(0.570)
N	1,385	1,699	1,393
Include polynomial of Army goal as a control function?	Yes	Yes	Yes

NOTES: The table reports coefficient estimates from a regression relating the log number of high-quality enlistments per population to factors affecting enlistment supply. The regression is estimated using a two-stage approach described in Chapter Three; the first stage incorporates year and state fixed effects. The unit of observation is a state and quarter; the sample includes the 50 U.S. states during the period between Q1 1999 and Q2 2007. Standard errors clustered on state are reported in parentheses.

† Denotes statistical significance at the 10 percent level.

* Denotes statistical significance at the 5 percent level.

** Denotes statistical significance at the 1 percent level.

Figure 5.1
Estimated Percentage Change in Navy High-Quality Enlistments Due to a 10 Percent Change in the Ratio of Military to Civilian Pay

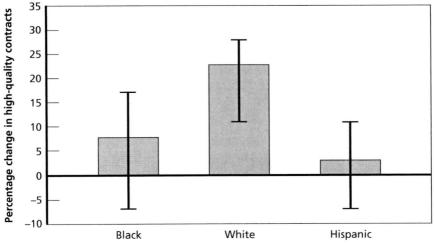

Figure 5.2
Estimated Percentage Change in Navy High-Quality Enlistments Due to a
10 Percent Change in Production Recruiters

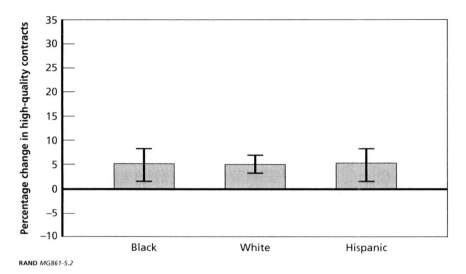

5.2 to 5.6 percent increase in enlistments. In the case of enlistment bonuses, the effects range from −0.7 to 0.9 percent. Thus, more differences are apparent across resources in terms of the magnitude of the effects than are apparent across market segments. Like the effects of pay, the effects of bonuses are not estimated with precision, except for the case of white enlistment supply. The imprecision of our estimates also precludes strong conclusions about the effects of educational incentives, although, in general, these incentives do not appear closely linked to high-quality Navy enlistments.

Effects of the Iraq War

Figure 5.4 plots the time series of the estimated Iraq residual for the Navy. The Army and Navy Iraq trajectories are most similar for whites, with a roughly linear decrease following the invasion culminating in an estimated war-related decrease in enlistments on the order of 30 to 40 percent by 2007. For minorities, in contrast, Army and Navy patterns are divergent. Whereas blacks were the group most negatively affected by Iraq in the Army, for the Navy the black Iraq residual is positive,

Figure 5.3
**Estimated Percentage Change in Navy High-Quality Enlistments Due to a
10 Percent Change in Mean Enlistment Bonus Amount**

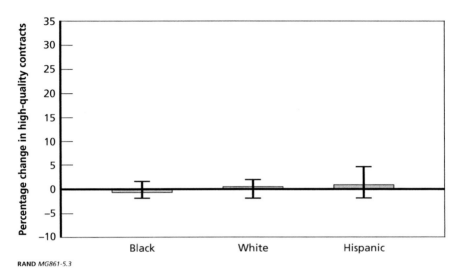

RAND *MG861-5.3*

albeit not statistically different from zero. For Hispanics, the Navy Iraq effect is positive, statistically significant, and stable at about 20 percent. One interpretation of this pattern is that it is a cross-service effect; given that Iraq war casualties have been concentrated among ground combatants, particularly in the Army and Marine Corps, individuals wishing to minimize their risk of injury or death while still joining the military may have substituted Navy service for Army or Marine Corps service.[1] Additionally, although Army deployments have increased substantially since 9/11, Navy deployments have remained relatively stable. Our simple model was specific to each service and did not account for the possibility of cross-service effects; one logical extension of this research suggested by Figure 5.4 would be to estimate a more complicated model in which the enlistment decision across services is considered jointly.

---

[1]   Between March 2003 and February 2009, there were 2,497 fatalities in Iraq among the active Army component, 897 among the active Marine component, and 82 among the active Navy component.

Figure 5.4
Estimated Effects of the Iraq War for the Navy, by Market Segment

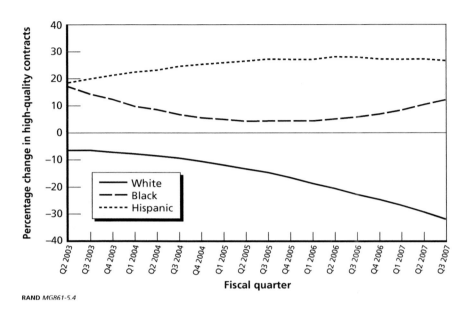

RAND *MG861-5.4*

Effects of the Unemployment Rate and Demographic Variables

In general, the effects of demographic variables are modest or not estimated with precision in the Navy model. We estimate changes in the
civilian economy, as captured by changes in the unemployment rate,
to have a small effect on Navy high-quality enlistments. A 10 percent change in the unemployment rate is associated with a 0.3 percent
change in high-quality white Navy enlistments. None of the estimated
effects of the college enrollment rate, the crime rate, or the adult obesity rate is statistically different from zero. The effect of the noncitizen
share is also small, except in the case of Hispanics, where we estimate a
positive association between noncitizen share and high-quality enlistments. Specifically, we estimate that a 10 percent increase in the noncitizen share of the population increases Navy Hispanic enlistments by
4.2 percent.

Effects of Goals

Figure 5.5 plots the relationship between Navy goals and contracts analogous to the results presented in Figure 4.11 for the Army. For the Navy, goals range between 8 and 214 high-quality contracts per 100,000 population per quarter, although, for most states, the goals lie near the Navy average of 51. The figure reveals that, at the goal levels typically observed between 1999 and 2007, minority representation increases at the margin as goals are increased. For states with more modest goals of 40 and below, the largest observed increases occur among blacks, while Hispanics achieve the largest representation gains at goal levels between 40 and 110 per 100,000. As with the Army, at very high goal levels, augmentation of goals is not associated with additional contracts, suggesting that, in many locations, goals are already set at levels sufficiently high so as to elicit maximal recruiter effort. In contrast to the Army, for the Navy, goal increases are associated with increased numbers of contracts even at very low goal levels.

Figure 5.5
Estimated Percentage Change in Navy High-Quality Enlistments Associated with a Unit Change in Goals, at Varying Goal Levels

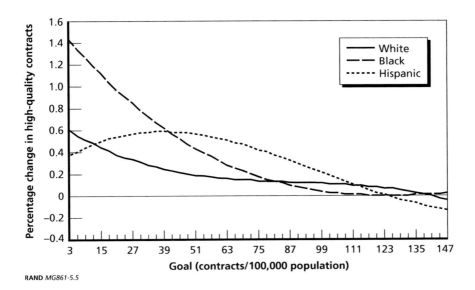

Accounting for Recent Changes in Minority Representation

The representation of Hispanics among high-quality Navy contracts increased dramatically, by 5.3 percentage points, between Q4 2002 and Q4 2005, from 10.9 percent to 16.2 percent. A key question is what factors explain this increase in representation. To what extent is this increase due to changes in Navy resources, demographic factors, or the Iraq war?

To decompose this national change, we follow the same procedure used for the Army to create Table 4.5. As described in Chapter Four, for each explanatory factor, we use the coefficient estimates for the Navy to recalculate expected high-quality enlistments under the assumption that this factor had remained constant at its Q4 2002 level through Q4 2005. We then estimate the contribution of this factor to the increase between 2002 and 2005 by comparing the expected enlistments to actual enlistments. As noted in the case of the Army, the contribution of a given factor reflects the relative responsiveness of different market segments to each incentive and the magnitude and direction of changes in the factor. Because we are focusing on the Hispanic share of high-quality enlistments, how a given factor affects white and black high-quality enlistments also plays a role in determining the contribution of a factor. The results of the decomposition of the increase in Hispanic enlistments are reported in Table 5.2.

The decomposition reveals that the Iraq war variables are key variables explaining the increase in Hispanic representation between 2002 and 2005 in the Navy. Recall from Figure 5.4 that the Iraq war was associated with an increase in Hispanic and black enlistments in the Navy and a decline in white enlistments. As white enlistments declined due to the Iraq war, Hispanic representation increased. The underlying reason for the positive relationship between the Iraq war and Hispanic and black Navy enlistments is unclear. As noted above, one possible explanation is that blacks and Hispanics who preferred to join the military switched from the Army, where we find a negative relationship between Hispanic and black enlistments and the Iraq war, toward the Navy. The Navy has experienced far fewer casualties than

Table 5.2
Decomposition of Navy Hispanic High-Quality Representation Between Fiscal Years 2002 and 2005

Explanatory Factor	Explained Change (%)
Iraq war	5.0
Noncitizen population share	0.4
Bonuses	0.4
Recruiters	0.4
Relative military pay	−0.4
Navy College Fund	0.2
MGIB	−0.6
Other	−0.9
Total change predicted by model	4.5
Total actual change	5.3
Unexplained	0.8

the Army and may be viewed as a "safer" service by black and Hispanic youth. Another possibility is that the nature of Navy service changed after 2003 and the onset of the Iraq war and that these changes were relatively more appealing to black and Hispanic enlistments than to white recruits to the Navy. Further research is needed to clarify the underlying causes of these results.

Cost Calculations

We combined OSD accounting data on costs with our effect estimates to calculate the predicted change in enlistments associated with a $1 million additional investment in Navy recruiters, enlistment bonuses, or military pay.[2] The limitations and caveats described for the Army cost estimates in Chapter Four also apply to these results.

Between 2000 and 2007, the Navy spent approximately $320 million per year on recruiter compensation and an additional $80 million for recruiter support, or $100,000 per recruiter. Enlistment bonus expenditures averaged $90 million each year. Based on these cost numbers, an additional $1 million expenditure would increase recruiters by 0.2 percent and bonuses by 1.1 percent. Table 5.3 reports the estimated changes in high-quality enlistments by market segment associated with such an expansion of resources.

Table 5.3 reveals that recruiters and pay provide similar numbers of enlistments, given the uncertainty of these estimates, but that recruiters appear to engender a more diverse recruit workforce. Using recruiters results in about 30 percent minority enlistments ([5 + 4]/30) while pay results in only about 10 percent ([3 + 1]/40) nonwhite enlistments. In contrast to the Army, the cost-effectiveness of enlistment bonuses lags behind the other resources in the Navy, with an estimated marginal cost of $76,800, more than double that of the other resources. Bonuses

Table 5.3
Navy Marginal Cost Estimates: Total New High-Quality Enlistments Associated with $1 Million Additional Spending on Incentives

	Enlistment Bonus	Recruiters	Regular Military Compensation
White	10	21	36
Black	0	5	3
Hispanic	3	4	1
Total	13	30	40
Cost per recruit[a]	76,800	33,600	28,500

[a] The marginal cost of regular military compensation is computed as the number of new enlistments associated with an additional $1 million.

---

[2] Because the effects of our educational variables are so imprecisely estimated, we cannot draw reliable conclusions regarding the effects of these incentives, so we omit them from the cost analysis.

are costly in the Navy because they generate relatively few enlistments, 13 versus 30 and 40 for recruiters and pay, respectively, for an additional $1 million expenditure of resources, according to our estimates. Given the lack of evidence in the Navy data that blacks respond to enlistment bonuses, it is also unsurprising that increases in bonuses are predicted to generate predominantly white enlistments.

The results in Table 5.3 and from the cost estimates in Chapter Four indicate that, in both the Army and Navy, recruiters are a fairly attractive resource in terms of obtaining a diverse workforce at a reasonable cost.

CHAPTER SIX

Conclusions and Policy Implications

A key question motivating this report is what factors explain the large drop in black representation among Army enlistments in recent years and what policy measures might be taken to improve black enlistments. Similarly, the Navy has experienced an improvement in Hispanic representation, and a key question is what has explained this success and what measures might be taken to maintain this success. Minority representation among enlistments is an ongoing concern among policymakers who care about whether the all-volunteer force represents the society it defends. At the same time, steep declines in enlistments in a market segment for which the service has had past success, specifically black enlistments in the Army, are troublesome in light of the Army's continued requirements for high-quality enlistments in a challenging recruiting environment. For the Army to meet its recruiting mission with high-quality enlistments, it needs to identify problem areas with key market segments and attempt to reverse such trends. In this chapter, we summarize our key conclusions and policy implications of this report with respect to these questions.

Factors Explaining Trends in Minority Representation

Black representation among Army enlistments fell 8.3 percentage points, from 18.9 percent to 10.6 percent, between 2000 and 2004, but rose 2.1 percentage points between 2005 and 2007. With respect to the 9.6 percentage point drop, our analysis suggests that this change reflects both the challenges of the recruiting environment due to the large negative effect of the Iraq war on black enlistments and the success of the Army in recruiting high-quality youth among the Hispanic and white populations. That is, because representation is measured as a share of high-quality enlistments, more success with one market segment means less success with another segment. More specifically, of the 8.3 percentage point drop, 5.2 percentage points were due to the greater negative effect of the Iraq war on black enlistments than white or Hispanic enlistments in the Army. The Iraq war was associated with a negative effect for all three market segments, but the effect was largest for blacks, explaining a 45 percent drop in high-quality enlistments for blacks versus a 21 percent drop for whites and Hispanics over our data period. On the other hand, black enlistments were more insensitive to the large increases in regular military compensation relative to civilian pay that occurred over this period, compared with white and Hispanic enlistments. Consequently, 2.0 percentage points of the decline in black representation are due to increases in the Hispanic and white enlistments, and therefore market share, relative to black enlistments. Other factors also affected black representation over the 2000–2004 period, but the Iraq war and relative military compensation were the key factors.

Over the period 2005 to 2007, black representation among Army high-quality enlistments increased. Again, the Iraq war was a key factor, but the role of the Iraq war was positive, not negative, as in the earlier period. Specifically, of the 2.1 percentage point increase, 2.3 percentage points can be explained by the Iraq war residual.[1] Our model can explain this incongruity. In particular, our data indicate that Iraq had a large negative effect for blacks, but one that developed rapidly and stabilized by 2005. For white and Hispanic enlistments, the negative effects of Iraq expanded beyond 2005, leading to an increase in black share in the later period. On the other hand, the increases in military regular compensation relative to civilian pay continued to exert a stronger effect on white and Hispanic enlistments than black enlistments,

---

[1]   The role of the Iraq war is larger, 2.3 percentage points, than the entire change in black representation, 2.1 percentage points, because other factors had a negative role, partially offsetting the effects of the Iraq war.

resulting in a 1.2 percentage point decline in black representation over the same period. Thus, the weaker responsiveness of black youth to increases in relative pay has reduced black representation in the Army.

The decline in black representation among Army high-quality enlistments is in part due to the success of the Army in increasing Hispanic high-quality enlistments. We decomposed the 3.3 percentage point increase in Army Hispanic enlistments between 2000 and 2003 to better understand the factors underlying this change. Our analysis suggests that educational benefits, and specifically the increases in the MGIB benefit, explain about one-third of the 3.3 percentage point increase, or 1.4 percentage points. Increases in military pay, and the stronger responsiveness of Hispanic than black youth to increases in relative military pay, explain almost a quarter of the increase in Hispanic representation over this period. Since white Army enlistments are also highly responsive to increases in relative military pay, the increase in white enlistments had an offsetting effect on Hispanic representation. Thus, recent resource changes have been important in explaining improvements in Hispanic representation in the Army in recent years.

In contrast to the Army, black representation in the Navy has been relatively stable in recent years, while Hispanic representation among high-quality Navy enlistments has increased. Specifically, Hispanic representation rose 5.3 percentage points between 2002 and 2005. We find that the majority of this increase—5 percentage points—is explained by the positive estimated effect of the Iraq war on Hispanic enlistments in our model. We estimate that the Iraq war has had a larger positive effect on Hispanic than black enlistments, and a negative effect on white enlistments. Thus, as the Iraq war progressed over this period, the Hispanic share rose dramatically in response. The underlying cause of the Iraq war's positive effects for black and Hispanic Navy recruiting is unclear. One possibility is that minority youth who would like to serve in the military are choosing the Navy over the Army. However, other explanations are also possible. For example, preferences for Navy service among different market segments may have changed during this period, perhaps due to the Iraq war but also perhaps due to other changes during this period in the Navy, such as changes in Navy missions as the Navy reduced its force size. Such changes in preferences may have resulted in a reduction in white enlistments, all else equal, but an increase in Hispanic and black enlistments.

Looking Forward

The Effects of the Iraq War

Looking to the future, the data suggest that the Army has largely already experienced most of the expected decline in black high-quality enlistments related to the Iraq war and that the war will account for less variation in black high-quality enlistments going forward. The extent to which minority enlistments respond to the drawdown of operations in Iraq remains an open question. One possibility is that the decline in enlistments associated with the Iraq war is temporary and will reverse as operations change. On the other hand, the decline might be permanent if positive attitudes toward the Army have permanently declined. Similarly, the positive effect on Navy enlistments among Hispanics and blacks as a result of the Iraq war may continue or reverse as operations there draw down, depending on whether attitudinal shifts toward the Navy are permanent.

Policy Options for Recruiting Minorities

Our analysis also provides information on the effects of alternative policies for recruiting black and Hispanic youth for the Army and Navy. In general, we find that the effects of resources differ more across market segments in the Army than in the Navy. That is, the effects of resources are quite similar across market segments in the Navy, but less so for the Army. The differences in the Army across market segments in the responsiveness to some resources suggest the possibility that resources could be targeted to specific market segments, or that decisions to change some resources might account for the differential effect on different segments.

More specifically, to increase black high-quality enlistments, the estimates suggest that expenditures on recruiters and enlistment bonuses yield more enlistments than comparable expenditures on military pay and educational benefits, although the effects of these latter two resources on black Army enlistments are not estimated precisely. For the Navy, the estimates suggest that recruiters also increase black Navy high-quality enlistments more than the other resources we considered, though the effects of the other resources were generally not statistically different from zero. For Hispanic Army enlistments, the estimates indicate that high-quality Hispanic youth are highly responsive to military pay. They are also responsive to Army educational benefits and recruiters and less responsive to Army enlistment bonuses. We did not consider the skill-channeling effects of bonuses and their relative effects on channeling different segments into hard-to-fill skill areas. In the Navy, we estimate high-quality Hispanic enlistments to be responsive to recruiters. The estimated effects of bonuses, military pay, and educational benefits are not statistically different from zero. Finally, to increase white high-quality enlistments, our analysis indicates that enlistments in both the Army and Navy are highly responsive to relative military pay, with recruiters in both services also estimated to have a large effect relative to bonuses and educational benefits.

The analysis suggests that decisions about how resources are allocated across recruiting policies—including bonuses, educational benefits, recruiters, and pay—will affect not just the number of high-quality enlistments but also the representation of different market segments. On the one hand, the services might consider targeting resources to specific market segments, based on the relative responsiveness of different market segments. On the other hand, such targeting may run counter to service beliefs about equity and fairness. For example, targeting educational benefits toward Hispanics might run counter to beliefs that such resources should be marketed to all segments equally. That said, the services should recognize that decisions about resources can affect representation. Thus, when considering whether to expand military pay versus the number of recruiters, the Army should recognize that a decision to focus on pay may increase Hispanic representation more than black representation. To the extent that the Army wants to increase black representation, increases in recruiters may be a wiser choice. More generally, resource-allocation decisions are likely to affect not only the size and cost of the future military, but also its representativeness.

Bibliography

ABC News and the *Washington Post*, ABC News/*Washington Post* Monthly Poll, April 2005.

———, ABC News/*Washington Post* Monthly Poll, June 2005.

Alvarez, Lizette, "Army Giving More Waivers in Recruiting," *New York Times*, February 14, 2007. As of March 19, 2009:
http://www.nytimes.com/2007/02/14/us/14military.html

Arkes, Jeremy, and M. Rebecca Kilburn, *Modeling Reserve Recruiting: Estimates of Enlistments*, Santa Monica, Calif.: RAND Corporation, MG-202-OSD, 2005. As of March 19, 2009:
http://www.rand.org/pubs/monographs/MG202/

Asch, Beth J., Christopher Buck, Jacob Alex Klerman, Meredith Kleykamp, and David S. Loughran, *Military Enlistment of Hispanic Youth: Obstacles and Opportunities*, Santa Monica, Calif.: RAND Corporation, MG-773-OSD, 2009. As of March 19, 2009:
http://www.rand.org/pubs/monographs/MG773/

Asch, Beth, James Hosek, and John Warner, "New Economics of Manpower in the Post–Cold War Era," in Todd Sandler and Keith Hartley, eds., *Handbook of Defense Economics, Vol. 2*, Amsterdam: Elsevier, 2007, pp. 1076–1138.

Binkin, Martin, and Mark Eitelberg, with Alvin Schexnider and Marvin Smith, *Blacks and the Military*, Washington, D.C.: Brookings Institution, 1982.

Bohn, Donald, and Edward Schmitz, *The Expansion of the Navy College Fund: An Evaluation of the FY 1995 Program Impacts*, Arlington, Va.: Navy Recruiting Command, 1996.

College Board, *Trends in College Pricing*, Washington, D.C., 1998–2008.

Dale, Charles, and Curtis Gilroy, "Determinants of Enlistments: A Macroeconomic Time-Series View," *Armed Forces and Society*, Vol. 10, 1984, pp. 192–210.

Dertouzos, James N., *Recruiter Incentives and Enlistment Supply*, Santa Monica, Calif.: RAND Corporation, R-3065-MIL, 1985. As of March 19, 2009:
http://www.rand.org/pubs/reports/R3065

————, *Cost-Effectiveness of Military Advertising: Evidence from 2002–2004*, Santa Monica, Calif.: RAND Corporation, DB-565-OSD, 2009. As of March 19, 2009:
http://www.rand.org/pubs/documented_briefings/DB565/

Dertouzos, James N., and Steven Garber, *Is Military Advertising Effective? An Estimation Methodology and Applications to Recruiting in the 1980s and 90s*, Santa Monica, Calif.: RAND Corporation, MR-1591-OSD, 2003. As of March 19, 2009:
http://www.rand.org/pubs/monograph_reports/MR1591/

Federal Bureau of Investigation, Uniform Crime Reports, various years. As of March 19, 2009:
http://www.fbi.gov/ucr/ucr.htm

Gates Commission—*See* President's Commission on an All-Volunteer Armed Force, *The Report of the President's Commission on an All-Volunteer Armed Force*, Washington, D.C.: U.S. Government Printing Office, 1970.

Heckman, James, and Salvador Navarro-Lozano, "Using Matching, Instrumental Variables, and Control Functions to Estimate Economic Choice Models," *Review of Economics and Statistics*, Vol. 86, No. 1, 2004, pp. 30–57.

Hosek, James, and Christine E. Peterson, *Enlistment Decisions of Young Men*, Santa Monica, Calif.: RAND Corporation, R-3238-MIL, 1985. As of March 19, 2009:
http://www.rand.org/pubs/reports/R3238/

Kilburn, M. Rebecca, "Minority Representation in the U.S. Military," University of Chicago, Department of Economics, unpublished manuscript, November 1992.

Kilburn, M. Rebecca, and Jacob Alex Klerman, *Enlistment Decisions in the 1990s: Evidence from Individual-Level Data*, Santa Monica, Calif.: RAND Corporation, MR-944-OSD/A, 1999. As of March 19, 2009:
http://www.rand.org/pubs/monograph_reports/MR944/

Kleykamp, Meredith, "College, Jobs, or the Military? Enlistment During a Time of War," *Social Science Quarterly*, Vol. 87, No. 2, 2006, pp. 272–290.

McFadden, David, "Econometric Analysis of Qualitative Response Models," in Zvi Griliches and Michael Intrilligator, eds., *Handbook of Econometrics, Vol. 2*, Amsterdam: Elsevier, 1983.

Murray, Michael, and Laurie L. McDonald, *Recent Recruiting Trends and Their Implications for Models of Enlistment Supply*, Santa Monica, Calif.: RAND Corporation, MR-847-OSD/A, 1999. As of March 19, 2009:
http://www.rand.org/pubs/monograph_reports/MR847/

Negrusa, Sebastian, John Warner, and Curtis Simon, "Effects of a School Subsidy on College Attendance: The Case of the Montgomery GI Bill," unpublished manuscript, Santa Monica, Calif.: RAND Corporation, 2007.

Plümper, Thomas, and Vera E. Troeger, "Efficient Estimation of Time-Invariant and Rarely Changing Variables in Finite Sample Panel Analyses with Unit Fixed Effects," *Political Analysis*, Vol. 15, No. 2, 2007, pp. 124–139.

Senate Committee on Armed Services, Report 93-884, 1974.

Simon, Curtis J., and John T. Warner, "Managing the All-Volunteer Force in a Time of War," *Economics of Peace and Security Journal*, Vol. 2, No. 1, 2007, pp. 20–29.

SurveyUSA, Job Approval Polls: President of the United States, 2005–2006. As of March 19, 2009:
http://www.surveyusa.com/index.php/surveyusa-poll-results/

Tyson, Ann Scott, "Army Having Difficulty Meeting Goals in Recruiting," *Washington Post*, February 21, 2005. As of March 19, 2009:
http://www.washingtonpost.com/wp-dyn/articles/A40469-2005Feb20.html

U.S. Census Bureau, Current Population Survey, various years. As of March 19, 2009:
http://www.census.gov/cps/

Warner, John, Curtis Simon, and Deborah Payne, *Enlistment Supply in the 1990s: A Study of the Navy College Fund and Other Enlistment Incentive Programs*, Defense Manpower Data Center, DMDC Report No. 2000-015, 2001.